# ZEN OR THE FLOWER OF BUDDHISM

# ZEN OR THE FLOWER OF BUDDHISM

M. J. de Mallac

The Book Guild Ltd
Sussex, England

First published in Great Britain in 2003 by
The Book Guild Ltd
25 High Street
Lewes, East Sussex
BN7 2LU

Typesetting in Times by
Acorn Bookwork, Salisbury, Wiltshire

Printed in Great Britain by
Bookcraft (Bath) Ltd, Avon

A catalogue record for this book is available from
The British Library.

ISBN 1 85776 679 2

*To Deisetz T. Suzuki, Reginald H. Blyth,*
*Thomas Merton and Alan Watts.*
'In memoriam'

If you do not get it from yourself,
Where will you go for it?

Old poem in the *Zentin Kushi*


For though the word 'Zen' is
Japanese and though Japan is now
its home, Zen Buddhism is the
creation of T'ang dynasty China (618–907).

Alan Watts


The real way to study Zen is to
penetrate the outer shell and
taste the inner kernel which cannot be defined.

Thomas Merton

# CONTENTS

# PREAMBLE

Dealing with a topic of such noetic quality as Zen with which, incidentally, we claim some familiarity over the years, calls for a preliminary remark in that however fascinating the study of Zen, the point is not losing oneself in a purely theoretical way while, by the same token, overlooking or forgetting the spiritual practice involved at the heart of it on the path to enlightenment. After all, Buddha is the Sanskrit word for 'awakened one', hence referring to Gautama Siddharta or Shakya-muni Buddha, the historical Buddha traditionally personificating the state of enlightenment or awakening, that is, an inner transformation going, as we will see, beyond the world of psychology as implying *prajna* or intuitive wisdom, seeing into the realm of ultimate reality. However, before proceeding any further, let it be said that this essay has been brought to fruition, not under the guidance of a Zen Master or Roshi, rather as the result of a personally accrued reflection having all along, as it were, seeped through that layer of consciousness acting as storehouse, and this within the spirit of *muchoku* (non-profit).

Within this view we are led onto the pedigree of Zen. As is well-known, Zen is an abbreviation of the Japanese word *Zenno* or *Zena*, derived from the Chinese word *Ch'anna* or *Ch'an* for short, itself a transliteration of the Sanskrit *dhyana* usually translated as 'meditation'. Yet, as Alan Watts[1] has pointed out, this is a misleading translation because to us Westerners

1

meditation means little more than deep thought and reflection, whereas in Yoga psychology *dhyana* is a high state of consciousness in which man finds union with Ultimate Reality. For his part, Deisetz T. Suzuki[2] retains our attention upon submitting that though the term *zen* or *zenna* is the transliteration from the Sanskrit *dhyana*, it is far from emphasizing the latter, which is generally translated as 'meditation', or a 'concentrated state of consciousness', whereas what Zen proposes is not to make us realize this, but to bring about the awakening of a higher spiritual power so as to come directly into contact with reality itself. As already intimated, this power or *prajna* in Sanskrit – translated in Chinese as *pan-jou* and in Japanese as *hannya* – is the highest form of intuition we humans are in possession of.

Suzuki is quite emphatic about it: Zen is not *dhyana* but *prajna*. So much so that although according to tradition Bodhidharma – who came to China in 527 – is regarded as the first Patriarch of the Indian lineage of Zen in this country, in reality the Zen school of Buddhism started with Hui-neng (Wei-lang; Jap: Eno, 638–713). It was Hui-neng who for the first time laid the foundation for the idea that the Buddhist life consists in awakening *prajna*-intuition and not in disciplining oneself in *dhyana* exclusively.

As the author explains elsewhere[3], Bhodidharma and the four succeeding Patriarchs did not make any distinction between *prajna* and *dhyana*, so much so that in their practice of Zen there was no differentiation between the two, but the sixth Patriarch, Hui-neng, revolutionized the approach to Zen in that, as the originator or founder of Zen Buddhism, he emphasized *prajna* instead of *dhyana*. The drift of it is that the former is not something which comes out of the latter

2

but that *dhyana* itself is *prajna*. In other parlance, *prajna* is something which is to be obtained by perfecting oneself in *dhyana* exercise, and it underlies every experience we have. *Dhyana* must be awakened to *prajna*.

There is however a wider recognition at this point, namely that the current use of the substantive Zen ought to be appraised as Zen insight instead, the import thereof admittedly of the most unusual yet sustainable type. To wit, the view of Thomas Merton[4] in that Zen is not an ideology nor a worldview; neither a theology nor a mystique; neither a way to ascetic perfection nor mysticism *per se*. In short, Zen is no convenient category of ours at all. In fact, any attempt to tag it contrarily to its spirit proves incongruous. Zen, says the author, 'cannot be properly judged as a mere doctrine, for though there is in it implicit doctrinal elements, they are entirely secondary to the inexpressible Zen experience.'

Why, in this connection very serious and responsible practitioners of Zen reportedly go as far as denying that it is a school, even turning down that it is confined to Buddhism and its structural organization. In this respect, we can note here that the famed Zen Master Dogen Zenji (1200–53) went as far as saying categorically that anybody who would regard Zen as a school or a sect of Buddhism and call it as such is a devil! This relates, by the way, to what Merton[4] has articulated further on, that is, to regard Zen merely and exclusively as Zen Buddhism is to falsify it and, by the same token, betray the fact that 'one has no understanding of it whatever.' And again, this does not mean that there cannot be 'Zen Buddhism', but Zen-men will realize the difference between their Buddhism and their Zen – 'even while admitting that for them Zen is in fact the purest expression of Buddhism'.

This way of thinking is consistent with what Watts[5] has remarked earlier on, namely that although historically Zen is an aspect of Buddhism, yet in itself it is so vital and elusive that it escapes definition. To be understood it must be lived. For living Zen, as distinct from academic Zen, is 'above all process of unlearning, of the abandonment of ideology, of all fixed forms of thought and feeling whereby the mind tries to grasp its own life.' The message is clear: Zen is alive and cannot be analyzed. Whoever writes about Zen can never explain, he can only indicate, point out. Elsewhere[6], Watts has it that because the word Zen indicates a very spiritual state of full liveness and non-grasping, it is really impossible to define Zen.

The foregoing is not foreign to the understanding of Karlfried von Dürckheim[7], for whom any verbal or written statement about Zen remains quite a problem for the outside observer, unless its teaching be constantly in keeping with the living experience from which it derives and leads to. It follows that such a teaching is worth its mettle as long as it is proving conducive to the conditions and results expected of it. Zen teaching brings out the most in us as living experience, not in theory but through practice based on a sound and intimate experience leading to it. Zen is not a theoretical essentialism but an essential practice, the meaning and import of which being our awakening to one's original or true Buddha nature – in Western parlance, the meeting of man with his own Being, hence his transformation through it as his most precious gift, yet upon the evidence that each of us has to find it out for himself.

Zen is simply not a religion or a philosophy, writes

Sohaku Ogata[8], it is something else: Life itself. It thus implies that the essential spirit of Zen is alive, dynamic, non-conformist and non-traditionalist. One doesn't understand Zen, one lives it concretely through awakening or enlightenment along, no doubt, a spiritual path quite its own as brought about by what von Dürckheim has implied just now, that is, self-transformation.

There is room for further exploration of the question, namely, of 'What is Zen?' Granted that the pedigree of Zen goes back to the T'Ang dynasty in China following the mutation of Indian Buddhism, the answer is given by Suzuki in a nutshell here: Zen is discipline in enlightenment. The latter, also known as awakening, means emancipation, and emancipation is no less than freedom. The real freedom is the outcome of enlightenment. In fact, it is Zen that makes most of enlightenment or awakening. In as much as Zen is the most significant human experience, one must resort to language to express it to others as well as to oneself. But Zen verbalism has its own features, which violate all rules of linguistics. In Zen, experience and expression are one. Zen verbalism expresses the most concrete experience.

Suzuki goes on to say that Zen discipline consists in attaining enlightenment, the latter finding a meaning hitherto hidden in our daily concrete particular experience, such as eating, drinking or business of all kinds. The meaning thus revealed is something not added from outside. It is in being itself, in becoming itself, in living itself. This, in Japanese, is called a life of *kono-mama* or *sono-mama* meaning the 'isness' of a thing. Zen does not indulge in abstraction or in conceptualization at all. At this point, let it be said that the clue to the nature of the issue is that Zen boasts of four

5

widely acknowledged 'pregnant characteristics' leading to what has been intimated earlier on, namely, an inner transformation beyond dualism and the opposites (topics dealt with later on); a special transmission outside the orthodox Buddhist scriptures; non-dependency on words or letters; direct pointing to the Being of man; seeing into one's true or original nature; and attainment of Buddhahood. After all, the man of Zen, far from being a sort of superman, is reportedly an ordinary, awakened, accomplished and level-headed individual akin to what that old sage, Chuang-tzu (c.369–286 BCE) described as 'The true man of no title.'

# THE GIST OF IT

While the evidence speaks thus far for itself, at least to our way of thinking, it affords credibility as bears coherence once again to Merton[10] for whom Zen is the very awareness of life living itself in us. Zen falls outside all particular structures and distinct forms; it is neither opposed to them nor not opposed to them. It neither denies them nor affirms them, loves them or hates them, rejects them or desires them. Zen is consciousness unstructured by particular forms or particular systems, a transcultural, trans-religious, transformed consciousness. Zen is not only beyond the formulation of Buddhism but also in a certain way 'beyond' (and even pointed to by) the revealed message of Christianity, says Merton. It follows that to define Zen in terms of religious system or structure would miss it completely. Zen is not something to be grasped, nor understood by being set apart in its own category, separated from anything else. Zen is not a one-dimensional proposition, and cannot be grasped as long as one remains passively conformed to any cultural or social imperatives, whether ideological, sociological or what have you. Zen implies a breakthrough, an explosive liberation from one-dimensional conformism, a recovery of unity which is not the suppression of opposites but a simplicity beyond them (more about this further on).

It is true that in the case of Watts[5], Zen – as the essential experience underlying Buddhism – is not a 'what'; it is not a thing, which is to say an aspect of experience definable by a word or concept. Zen is close to the non-verbal, non-symbolic, and totally undefinable world of the concrete as distinct from the abstract. In fact, from the outset Zen dispenses with all forms of theorization, doctrinal instruction and lifeless formality. What one is talking about here is a vigorous attempt to come into direct contact with the truth itself without allowing theories and symbols to stand between the knower and the known. The truth is that Zen is so hard to understand; just because it is so obvious, and we miss it time and time again because we are looking for something obscure. What is implied at this stage is that with our eyes on the horizon we do not see what lies at our feet. The truth is that in Zen, as in life, there is nothing at all which one can hold to and say: 'This is it, I have got it.' Therefore, pursues Watts in his own words, any book on Zen is rather like a mystery story with the last chapter missing; there is always something which escapes definition, which can never be expressed in words, and however hard we may try to catch up with it, it is one place ahead.

Later on there has been the testimony of Toshihito Izutsu[11] to the effect that Zen abhors all forms of intellectualism, verbalism or conceptualization, not to speak of those random thoughts and ideas that constantly arise and dart about in the mind to perturb its serenity. What the author is driving at is that reasoning or thinking, in whatever form it takes place, always involves the 'I' or ego entity (more about this in due course) becoming conscious of something. As basic structure of consciousness of, it follows that both the thinking ego and the subject of thinking are separated from one another, or standing against one another. The consciousness is dualism (here again, a topic for

8

further elaboration). But what Zen is concerned with above everything else is the actualization of 'consciousness' pure and simple, not 'consciousness of'. This is a moot point on the ground that, although similar in verbal form, 'consciousness-pure-and-simple' and 'consciousness-of' are worlds apart in that the former is an absolute or metaphysical awareness without the thinking subject and without the object of thought. It is not our awareness of the external world; rather, the whole world of Being becoming aware of itself in us and through us, says Izutsu.

This ensures some help in considering for instance the next step, that is, what of those who have been awakened or enlightened? They do not remain permanently in a state of 'mental void and silence'. Quite the contrary in that they are in complete possession of their faculties, which they exercise freely and spontaneously. As regards their thinking, though, it is noteworthy that it unfolds itself at a totally different level of consciousness from that with which one is familiar in ordinary circumstances.

Judging from the above, what matters for Zen man primarily or exclusively is 'a direct experience of reality in its primordial non-differentiation', which in Zen terminology is often referred to as one's original Face even before one's parents were born (read what one is beyond the subject-object structure of one's ego-consciousness, after Richard De Martino, who we are going to come across later). What Izutsu infers is that the purity of the 'Original Face' is, as it were, contaminated by the differentiating activity of the discursive intellect; hence the natural abhorrence of Zen for all kinds of abstract and theoretical thinking.

# A MATTER PRIMARILY OF INSIGHT

While it is mandatory to safeguard the integrity of the issue presently under consideration – as having to admit that its appeal is of restrictive public interest – evidence, on the other hand, shows that many in the West of whatever professional calling have dealt authoritatively with the intricacies of Zen, hence proving quite useful to the mind tutored in the discipline. From a personal viewpoint, though, we feel that what is required from the outset is a concerted systematic approach, hence the lay-out of the present text in terms of perceptive observations and presentation of the subject matter not necessarily given to erudition. On the other hand, we take due notice that Zen sounds baffling to the lay reader, or that the general impression of Zen in the West is reportedly somewhat meddled, if not confused, despite the increasing interest it arouses. In fact, any adequate reckoning at this point would bear out that with Zen it practically suggests always 'something else in one's effort to gain further insight into the matter'. After all, one is dealing with an awareness of an expansion of consciousness (transformation might be a more suitable term for it) beyond all thought process. As Christmas Humphreys puts it[12], 'while the part sees the whole there is no Zen, for there are still two things, the part and the whole.' Moreover, being above all a live experience, non-verbal in character, 'Zen is simply not accessible to the purely literary and scholarly endeavour'.

Giving the discussion a broader aspect, Watts[13] remarks that to know what Zen is, and especially what it is not, there is no alternative but to practise it, to experiment with it in the concrete so as to discover its meaning which underlies the words. For the author, to interpret such a phenomenon as Zen there is a clear principle to be followed. On the one hand, it is necessary to be sympathetic and to experiment with the Zen way of life to the limit of one's possibilities. On the other hand, his controversial statement not to join the 'organization', hence not becoming involved with its institutional commitments, since the essential standpoint of Zen refuses to be organized, or to be made the exclusive possession of any institution. Moreover, 'if there is anything in this world which transcends the relativities of cultural conditioning, it is Zen by whatever name it may be called'. While we are in sympathy with Watts' view here, the spiritual, not the cultural, aspects of Zen serve as an attracting pole institutionally speaking, hence the choice of the majority of Zen adepts, not incidentally concerned whether many of the ancient exponents of Zen were never members of any organization, and 'never sought the acknowledgement of any formal authority.'

It remains to examine the issue in the light of further argument in that the Buddha himself is reported to have confided to his alleged favourite disciple, Ananda: 'Be lamps unto yourselves ... look not for refuge to any one beside yourself.' It follows that we personally do not represent ourself as Buddhist or 'Zenist' for that matter; rather as a student of Zen insight, the core of which equates with the flower or apotheosis of Buddhism beyond the possibility of ambivalence and misunderstanding to boot.

In fact, it has been judiciously remarked that the most characteristic difference between Zen and all the other philosophical, religious and mystical teachings is that, without getting away from daily life Zen, with all its concrete and practical aspects, harbours something else that allows it to stand away from the 'maddening crowd'. Like flowing water in its freshness, Zen constantly renews itself, hence is always actual, alive, recreating itself at every moment.

Such an assertion falls in line with Merton's description of Zen[10] as the awareness of pure being beyond subject and object as a result of enlightenment or awakening, or the resolution of all subject-object relationship and opposites in a pure void (more about this fundamental notion at a later stage). The author points out that the awareness in question is not reflexive, self-conscious, philosophical or theological in nature, but in some sense entirely beyond the scope of psychological observation and metaphysical reflection. In effect, one is dealing here with an awareness of purely spiritual quality which, in order to be preserved as such, cannot be rationalized nor verbalized in terms of inner experience: its central meaning cannot be conveyed, neither by thought nor words.

There is room for further elaboration of the issue in that, Zen claiming the teaching of Being (read, the equivalent of Ultimate Reality) in the view of von Dürckheim[7], it ensues that the insight thereof derives from the experience of Being and life through Being too, hence given neither to psychological nor philosophical reflection nor metaphysical speculations, incidentally in keeping with what Merton has inferred just now. Zen insight is the expression of inner experience, namely that of 'Being as our essential nature'. Such an experience is the effect, content, form of consciousness

12

called upon to be transformed by way of meditation. Zen insight follows experiencing one's essential nature or experiencing Being, since one's essential nature is the way Being manifests itself in us. This, pursues von Dürckheim, is the very experience on which hinges the aforesaid insight, or the very experience of one's own true nature permeated by self-realization through Being. 'It is the experience of Being within the specificity of our own essence. Being that we indeed are, beyond concept and image of what we consciously entertain.'

One's attention lies next in the attempt to deal with the origin of Zen insight, followed by *zazen* as the hub of it, then awakening or enlightenment (read, from *kensho* to *satori*) while, on both counts taking into account those pivotal elements coming into it: (i) within the appropriate conceptual framework, and (ii) as trans-cultural, trans-religious and transformed consciousness unique in its genre.

# THE ROARING SILENCE OF BUDDHA

Tradition has it that in the course of the Buddha's wordless Flower Sermon, during which he presented in silence a golden flower, the choice of his successor fell on Mahakasyapa because, contrarily to the other disciples, the latter was the only one among them to have understood the message of the Master simply upon smiling. In short, an acknowledged outstanding student of the historical Buddha and renowned for his ascetic discipline and moral strictness, Mahakasyapa (also known as Kasyapa or Kassapa) got the drift of it: the golden flower symbolizing ultimate things, one cannot speak of them, one can only be them. On the other hand, as pointed out by Watts[5], Gautama the Buddha (the Enlightened One) took great care to avoid any description of the illumination or awakening which he encountered while sitting one night under the giant fig-tree at Gaya in the fifth century BCE. Little wonder to be told that Zen insight originated at the moment when the Buddha attained his supreme insight into the mysteries of life, such an insight having passed from Mahakasyapa to the 28 Zen Patriarchs of the Indian lineage down to Bodhidharma (Chi: P'u-t'i-ta-mo or Tamo; Jap: Bodaidaruma or Daruma, c.470–443) who, as mentioned earlier on, introduced Zen teaching in China (read, in 527 CE). Seven centuries later, Dogen Zenji, acknowledged as the most important Zen Master of Japan, brought the tradition to his country. What it boils down to is that the Zen insight was transmitted

14

from Patriarch to Patriarch without any intermediary of scriptures or doctrinal teaching. In fact, it was a direct communication which passed immediately from mind to mind, as understandable only to each Patriarch far enough developed for the purpose. Another important remark at this point is that Gautama the Buddha reportedly never tired of saying that his doctrine (read, Dharma) was concerned only with the way to enlightenment or awakening, and never claimed it as a revelation of the latter.

# THE SILENT ILLUMINATION

The next topic to envisage here is that, in contrast to the Rinzai school (Ch: Lin Chi I-huan) going back to the famed Zen Master of the T'Ang dynasty, Rinzai Gegen (Ch: Kin Chi I Hsuan, ?–866), known for his violent method of training, and Zen Master Daie Soko (Ch: Ta Hui Tsung-Kao, 1089–1163) of the Sung dynasty with his characteristic *koan* exercise, we are dealing with that equally well-known meditative discipline *zazen* or the Silent Illumination (Ch: *mo chao*; Jap: *moku shô*). The latter, reportedly more amenable to Western mentality, comes under the Soto school (Ch: Tas'ao Tsung), introduced in Japan by Dogen Zenji in the wake of the two great Zen Masters of the T'Ang dynasty: Tung Shan Lieng Chieh (Jap: Tozan Ryokai, 807–869), and his disciple successor, Ts'ao Shan Pen Chi (Jap: Sozan Honjaku, 840–861). With this in mind, the Soto school emphasizes above everything else the importance of sitting in meditation, the underlying idea being that awakening or enlightenment can be achieved only through a total participation and transformation of the whole personality of the meditator.

Now, agreed that in meditation the path is indeed the goal, yet this very path is called upon to bring the consciousness of the meditator to a state in which he can come to the experience of inner liberation to an extraordinary degree. Yet *zazen* or sitting meditation is unique in its genre in that, as Izutsu observes[11], Dogen

16

Zenji saw in such a practice the very actualization of the Buddha nature itself, that is, the intrinsically undifferentiated oneness of Being. In fact, the highest principle of Zen established by the Master is that enlightenment and practice are exactly one and the same thing. However, sitting in such a situation is not merely a bodily posture; rather, the meditator through the highest degree of existential plenitude 'is the awareness of Being; he is a living crystallization point of universal Life.'

In the course of our enquiry we need not take into account the technique involved in *zazen*, its being better dealt with, and no doubt guided by a Zen Master or Roshi who has himself experienced awakening or enlightenment to an appreciable degree, if not profoundly so, yet not without reservation at this point. In effect Roshi Philip Kapleau[14] reminds us that *zazen* is to be distinguished from other forms of meditation which usually involve a visualization or putting into the mind of a concept, idea, or other thought pattern. To be more precise, we may evoke in turn the Hindu Bhakti, Indian Tantra, Tibetan Tantrism, Patanjali's Ashtanga Yoga, Jewish Kabbalah, Christian Hesychasm, Sufism, and so on. The drift of it is that during *zazen* the mind is one-pointed, stabilized and emptied of random, extraneous thoughts.

What remains in the balance at this stage is the comprehensive appraisal of those pivotal elements coming under *zazen* as such, be it to lend cogency to the issue. The ensuing illustration is a case in point.

*Anatta* implying elimination of the ego or 'I', or complete release from it, let us start with what the latter really stands for.

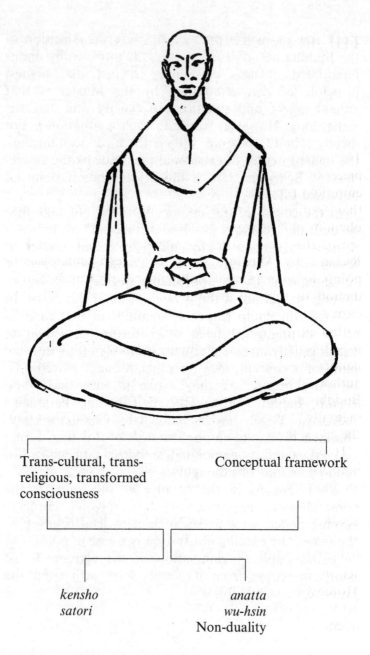

Trans-cultural, trans-
religious, transformed
consciousness

Conceptual framework

*kensho*
*satori*

*anatta*
*wu-hsin*
Non-duality

# THE BLIND SPOT OF CONSCIOUSNESS

The need is felt once again, then, to explore a vital piece of evidence which under the spell of the 'I', empirical ego, the little or small self is denounced as that artificial complex, that unstable and strange phenomenon beyond definition, that relative psycho-sensorial representation not amenable to analysis. For Richard De Martino[15], the 'I' or ego-consciousness points to an existential ambiguity, conflict and contradiction in that, at the limit, it is rent by a double cleavage within its very subject/object structure, split within as well as without, since 'never pure subject in its subjectivity, never absolutely free in its freedom, it is neither ground nor the course of itself.' Moreover, the author aptly remarks that Bodhidharma, and Zen Buddhism after him, realized that, finally and fundamentally, it is not that the ego has a problem, 'but that the ego is the problem'.

However, it behoves Robert Powell[16] to press the need for further explanation in that, as long as there is an individual 'I', it follows that the expression 'free will' is a contradiction in terms, for 'will', says he, can never be free, 'being simply another word for volition, or desire, which is always based on an idea'. It means that only when the ego has dissolved is there pure action, that is, action which is not the result of an idea. Moreover, in this state there is only action, without the actor, adds Powell, that action is timeless, 'and there is freedom, which is so total and absolute, not conditioned in any way because it is free from the net of time'.

Well-known for his attacks on the 'I' as separated from everything else, Watts has it that the so-called 'I' doesn't feel, think and smell in the sense of feeling, thinking and smelling at all because not separated from its own experience. The 'I' for Watts is that 'skin-encapsulated ego', hence neither substance nor entity, notwithstanding to be told elsewhere[13] that it is fundamental to every school of Buddhism that there is no ego, no enduring entity which is the constant subject of our experience. It means that the ego exists in an abstract sense alone, 'being an abstraction from memory' just, for instance, as the abstract path taken by the bird through the sky. In concrete reality, the bird left no line, and, similarly, 'the past from which the ego is abstracted has entirely disappeared.' The message is clear in that 'any attempt to cling to the ego or to make it an effective source of action is doomed to frustration.'

Earlier on we have the compelling observation of Aldous Huxley[17] to the effect that the 'I' is 'that dark little inspissated clot' affirming a separate me-substance while denying the fact that all existence is relationship and change. Robert Pirsig[18] steps in upon referring to the ego as 'this Cartesian Me', this 'little autonomous homunculus', this 'self-appointed editor of reality' as just an impossible fiction the moment we examine it closely. Ken Wilber takes the clue when he admits that 'The more I go into the I, the more I fall out of the I' or, as Swami Prabhavananda puts it even more to the point: 'Who do you think you are? Absolutely, basically, fundamentally, deep within you?'

Small wonder, then, that the 'I' has been labelled by Roshi Philip Kapleau as 'the blind spot of consciousness, that black magician, an abstraction release from the bind of illusion.' Moving on, Conrad Hyers[19] points to the artificiality and insubstantiality of the ego-mask hiding the true identity of the individual, notwithstanding the schizophrenia it engenders within the self and the world. Warwick Fox[20] makes no bones about it, namely the empowerment of the 'I' beginning and ending with the subject stuck in its constricted process (read, the ego-bound subject) cutting itself off from self-realization (more about it in a moment). As Zen Master Hakuin Zenji (Jap: Hakuin Ekaku, 1689–1769) had it, 'The cause of our sorrow is ego delusion.'

The quest for further evidence while we are at it comes from Matthieu Ricard[21] for whom the notion of the ego, the 'I', has no real existence at all as an autonomous and permanent entity. The ego or the 'I' exists neither in the mind nor in the body of the person, nor outside these, nor within their own make-up. The ego or the 'I' has no form, no colour, no localization whatever. The more one looks for it, the less one finds it. The individual 'I' is but a label stuck to an apparent continuity. It follows that the point is not to annihilate the ego, since it has never existed, but to denounce it as an impostor. At this stage, Ricard draws our attention that Buddhism proves instead the continuum or stream of consciousness within which the individual 'me' as permanent autonomous entity is firmly rejected (read, the doctrine of the non-ego or *anatta* following suit).

While what has been elaborated thus far proves consonant with our own stance, unfortunately the vast majority of people around us go on entertaining the notion of having an unalterable 'I' (Latin: *ego*), irrespective of the fact that it is a false perception based reportedly on a long chain of simple impressions which one has never experienced simultaneously. In

21

other parlance, most people will go on falling for the primacy of the 'I' or empirical ego despite the advocated wisdom of stepping out of it. In our view it would prove terribly difficult to convince people that the 'I' taken as reality cannot in any way reflect their true identity, nor does it point to their true nature.

A double question arises here, though: how to situate the 'I' or ego so much embedded in our Western mentality, and what of its liberation from bondage? We would put it this way: to begin with, neither substance nor entity, the 'I' is but the reflection here and now of the various yet ever-changing components of mental life such as emotions, moods, desires, will, hopes, memories, intention and so forth. Now, the ego-bound subject is stuck to his own constricted or encapsulated process; deprived of transpersonal disposition, there is no nurturing of the sense of self beyond self, no opening up to the wider, deeper sense of self; no search for the true self in both the psychological and spiritual sense; in other words, there is no self-realization. On the other hand, this is not the fate of such a one given to *prajna*-intuition, the practice of *zazen* or the inner experience of genuine meditation.

Grasping the issue by the right end is backed up by the doctrine of *anatta* or non-ego laid down, as is well-known, by the Mahayana or Great Vehicle school of Buddhism in the first century, hence considered to be the most important and characteristic feature of Buddhism. However, in contrast to the Hinayana or Small school of Buddhism, Suzuki[22] informs us that the latter has not gone beyond the negative statement of the doctrine in question, hence not carrying it to its logical consequences, to its limits. Mahayana, pursues our mentor, has not only extended the doctrine from its subjective significance to the objective world, but

22

has also boldly developed the positive conclusion implied in it. At any rate, in the case of *anatta* or the non-ego doctrine, both the Mahayanists and the Hinayanists deny that there is such thing as the ego substance behind our consciousness, as a concrete, simple, ultimate and independent unit.

Carrying the matter further, Suzuki tells us elsewhere[23] that the doctrine of the non-ego not only repudiates the idea of an ego substance but points to the illusiveness of the ego-idea itself. For the ego is something always eluding our grasp: 'when we think to have caught it, it is found to be no more than a slough left by the snake while the real ego is somewhere else.' The message is clear: 'The ego must be caught not from the outside but from within.'

# NO-MINDEDNESS

In our attempt to reach for further understanding, the notion of *wu-hsin* or No-Mindness comes to the fore. In effect, Hui-neng, sixth Patriarch of Ch'an (Zen) whom we have already come across, was notoriously known for the unique position he holds in the history of Zen, but is somehow famous for his advocacy of *wu-hsin* (Jap: *mushin*) or No-Mindedness in the practice of *zazen*. In short, contrarily to Hui-neng's predecessors, whose meditative discipline was one of duality, that is, looking at pure mind and receiving its light, meditation ought to be instead pure being alone, and not looking 'at' reality, but 'as' reality, and only so could the essence of things be realized by avoiding all qualities as pre-requisites to true seeing, in the words of Ernest Wood[24]. However, the alternative notion here is *wu-nien* or No-thought (read, thoughtlessness or idealessness or seeing and knowing things with the mind free of attachment), the term applied to meditation without thought or meditation on one's self-nature. Given more leeway here, the principle of *wu-nien* is related to *sunyata* (Void or Emptiness, to be dealt with later), for the true self-nature is characterized by this, so also related, as we will see subsequently, to *tathata* or Suchness, for self-nature cannot be known in terms of something else.

Admittedly, such compelling consideration calls for the testimony of others like Watts[13], for whom *wu-hsin* or *mushin* is a state of wholeness in which mind

24

functions freely and easily, without a sensation of a second mind or ego 'standing over with a club'. More explicitly submitted, Hui-neng insisted that the whole idea of purifying the mind was irrelevant and confusing, because one's nature is fundamentally clear and pure. In other words, pursues Watts, there is no analogy between consciousness or mind and a mirror that can be wiped, the reason being that the true mind is no-mind (*wu-hsin*). What the author is driving at is that mind is not to be regarded as an object of thought, as if it were a thing to be grasped and controlled. In all this, though, 'Hui-neng's teaching is that instead of trying to purify or empty the mind, one must simply let go of the mind because the mind is nothing to be grasped.'

In his endeavour to accommodate further evidence, Watts reminds us that the attitude of *wu-hsin* or *mushin* is by no means an intellectual exclusion of thinking, rather an action on any level of whatsoever, physical or psychic, without trying at the same moment to observe and check the action from outside. This attempt to act and think about the action simultaneously 'is precisely the identification of the mind with its idea itself'. In other words, we hear elsewhere[25] that '*wu-hsin* or *mushin* is when one's whole being seems as the head seems to the eyes – a transparent void, filled by all that one sees.'

Availing himself of another version, Izutsu[11] points out that what is meant by *wu-hsin* or No-Mindedness is not a purely negative state in which the mind has just ceased to function; rather, a peculiar state to be reached at the extreme limit of mindfulness, a state of apparent inaction brought about by an unusually inten- sified activity of the mind. Incidentally, what is to be understood here is an objectless thinking which is at the same time without a subject, that is, thinking subject: an objectless and subjectless thinking constituting the core of Zen meditation. In other parlance, what is actualized at this stage is 'neither I-and-Thou nor I-It, for there is no longer I as a subjective entity nor Thou or It as an objective entity'. Framed otherwise, when the core of Zen meditation is reached, the senser, the senses and the things sensed become one, hence meaning that the duality of the knower and the known, the inside and the outside, is transcended. A moot point to be borne in mind.

As variation on the same theme, we hear from Suzuki[26] that it is very difficult to find an English word corresponding to the term *wu-hsin* or *mushin*, and while 'unconsciousness' approaches it, the connotation is too psychological, notwithstanding that *wu-hsin* is decidedly an Oriental idea. To be free from mind-attachment, pursues the author, is somewhat circumlocutionary, but the idea is briefly to denote that state of consciousness in which there is no hankering, conscious or unconscious, after ego-substance, or a soul entity, or a mind as forming the structural unit of our mental life. As regards the attainment of this state of mind or *wu-hsin*, it means a mind free of all forms; it sees, says our mentor, into the fact that there is no difference between Buddhas and sentient beings: when once this state of *wu-hsin* or *mushin* is attained, it completes the Buddha life.

Interestingly enough, and while in no way exercising the hegemony of his stance, Suzuki has it next[27] it dawned on Hui-neng that, if Bodhidharma used the term *wu-hsin* for the Unconscious, Hui-neng replaced *hsin* by *nien*, bearing in mind that *wu-nien* is not mere forgetfulness here, or not remembering what one is doing; it is not a simple psychological term. When Hui-neng made the *wu-nien* the most fundamental fact of life in Zen, it corresponds to the Triple Emancipation: *sunyata* (Void or Emptiness), no form, and not striving. The term *wu-nien* is essentially Chinese. The offering of further reflection has it that *wu-hsin* or *mushin* belongs to an altogether different category. It is what makes up both the conscious and the unconscious; it is in them, with them, but it is more than both of them on account of its fundamental nature. Hence Suzuki's remark to the effect that 'the no-mind (*mushin*) is an inexhaustible reservoir of possibilities. When it is tapped, our consciousness gains power over in various ways: ethically, aesthetically, intellectually, and emotionally.'

Finally, calling on Humphreys[28], he emphasizes the point that *wu-hsin* – or the 'freedom of a mind that alights nowhere', or the mind that abides nowhere – is our true home, by which is meant the No-Mind before mind was born, or a state of consciousness before the division into duality created by thought takes place. In more pedestrian terms we are told that only a mind in the void is No-Mind, resting in the state of no-thinking or *mushin*, and only the mind that has reached such a stage for a second or an hour can know – and cannot speak of – the utter serenity and power that flow from Life itself into a mind that sets no barrier against it, we are told. Only then comes the nakedness of a mind newly cleaned of its self-wrought illusion.

# THE PRINCIPLE OF NON-DUALITY

If the initial task of ours is to look for evidence with a sustained openness of mind, then, surely, the principle of non-duality comes very much into the picture. So, besides being met in the *Advaita-Vedanta* under its most significant teacher, Sankara or Shankaracharya (788–820), the principle in question goes back to the Madhyamika or Middle Doctrine school of Buddhist philosophy too, the latter founded, as well-known, by Nagarjuna (c.100–200), himself duly acknowledged as its foremost representative, notwithstanding his status as the 14th Patriarch of the Indian lineage of Zen.

For our immediate purpose, though, the Madhyamika school claims that systems of thought based on dualism (read, the subject/object split, the whole and the part, being and non-being, enlightenment and non-enlightenment) cannot produce insight into the true nature of reality. To this end, Humphreys[28] observes that Zen functions in non-duality as opposed to the field of duality wherein the process of thought, of reasoning, discursive analysis takes place. To wit, what is sought after in Zen is not to be found by the intellect, still less in the realm of thought: it is beyond, behind, above the world of duality, however one views it. Moreover, whereas most disciplines have their being in a world of duality, Zen breaks through to non-duality, a personal, unmediated, direct experience. This is the sole and only purpose of all Zen effort, such an effort understood as coming from within. The message is clear: Zen functions in non-duality.

Judging from the foregoing, the following observa-

28

tions stand out. For one, no amount of thinking will achieve Zen in that in its very nature Zen lies beyond all thinking or other mental process in duality. Second, Zen is fully understood beyond the bi-polar field, with the reservation that such non-duality is akin to being 'not one, nor two, nor both nor neither'. Another version, coming from Powell[16], has it that the insight of non-duality is at the heart of the matter when it comes to understanding the Zen way, hence congruent with what has been intimated thus far, notwithstanding that it goes against the grain of our Western habit of thinking in dichotomous terms ever since the awakening of human consciousness; in short, our Cartesian consciousness.

Although we have dealt with the matter elsewhere[29], we have no qualms to repeat ourselves in view of lending cogency to the issue. The gist of it is that dualistic thinking is largely endemic in the West in the wake of such early thinkers as Empedocles, Aristotle, St Augustine of Hippo, St Thomas Aquinas – to name but those few – as has from its inception been entertained to this day by the Judeo-Christian and Islamic faiths, the Manichean and Gnostic so-called heresies coming into the picture for good measure. Or, as Watts has it[25], the Zoastrian brand of dualism has powerfully influenced the development of both Judaism and, even more, Christianity. Yet from the beginning of the fifth century BCE, the fall of Babylon to the Persians, to the end of the Crusades, 'the Mediterranean and European worlds were exposed to this influence in many different ways – through its infiltration of Greek religion, of Jewish apocalyptic literature, of Gnostic theologies, and through such daughter cults as Mithraism, Manicheism, and Catharism.'

Cartesianism, observed Henri-Frédéric Amiel[30], is a

most peculiar trait of the Latin world, its élites – bound to the fossilizing of their intellectual abstractions ("sic") are unable ... to penetrate the inner sanctum of life wherein ideas themselves are not divided, determined and shaped. Amiel emphasized the indelible nature of Cartesianism or dualistic thinking as the radical distinction of the subject/object, the deliberate isolation of self from other beings and things. In short, separated from nature and his cosmic roots, Cartesianism doesn't harbour universal life, the sense of the infinite, the intuition of the living unity within wholeness, nor does it cater for the mysteries of being.

In a wider yet no less explicit context, Cartesianism or dualistic thinking has, from the post-Socratics onwards, ever since led to a fragmented world view, hence the breaking up of the world into a multitude of separate entities and events. As such, our Western Cartesian heritage stands in direct opposition to the central tenets of Taoism, Hinduism and Buddhism (read, the unity of self and the world). Little wonder, then, that Cartesian man, his alienated self – perforce stranger to himself – seems condemned to miss the ground-source of his being, that is, his true or original Buddha nature. In effect, dualistic thinking in the form of fixation tends to lose sight of wholeness or unity of the All (more about which later).

We are confronted here with another piece of compelling evidence in that, in his evaluation of modern consciousness, Merton[4] points out that we have to take into account the still overwhelming importance of the Cartesian *cogito*, 'modern man, in so far as he is still Cartesian (he is of course going far beyond Descartes in many respects), is a subject for whom his own self-awareness as a thinking, observing, measuring and estimating "self" is absolutely primary.' Little wonder, then, that it is for man the indubitable 'reality', and all truths start right here. In other words, the more he is able to develop his consciousness as a subject over and against objects, the more he tends to isolate himself in his subjective prison, the more he finds himself a detached observer 'cut off from everything else in a kind of impenetrable alienated and transparent bubble which contains all reality in the form of purely subjective experience.'

In order to strike a sense of balance, other writers like, for instance, Robert Hamilton[31] have it that the absolute split between subject and object, mind and matter, body and soul propounded by philosopher René Descartes (1596–1650) as basic dualistic premise became imbedded – in fact, deeply so – in the general ethos of Western culture, that it would be very difficult to convince the majority of dualists among us to the contrary. For this author's predecessor, Aldous Huxley[32], Cartesianism has penetrated so deeply into the Western mind that it will be extraordinarily difficult to stop people from indulging into a falsified picture of the world, a stance, incidentally, in which physicist Werner Heisenberg assumes a conformity of view. A last observation off the cuff in that, in the opinion of Bede Griffiths, Cartesianism is the most disastrous error ever propagated in putting philosophy on a false trail for centuries, hence vitiating all modern thought.

The facts spelled out so far induce us to agree with them, notwithstanding their emphasis on evidence. On the other hand, one has to reckon with the acknowledged ontological, existential and epistemological frailty of such assumption Cartesianism begets. Yet the trouble is that most people will go on sticking to their Cartesian grids, hence, by the same token, permeating the contemporary cultural, philosophical and scientific climate,

31

there being no sign of abatement in view, and this – while not buying any purchase within the present postmodern era – for a long time to come. As Wilber[33] figures it, 'whereas Western tradition has been plagued, from its inception, with a series of brutal dualisms and that virtually all forms of Western philosophy have, right up to the present day, come to rest finally on one or the other of these dualisms, these and the root issue about them, cannot finally be solved by empiricism, nor rationalism, but finally by contemplation.'

Suzuki[34] steps in once again upon submitting that all duality is falsely imagined, on the plea that false imagination teaches that such things as light and shade, long and short, black and white are different and are to be discriminated. Yet evidence shows that they are not independent of each other; they are only different aspects of the same thing; they are terms of relation, not of reality. 'Conditions of existence are not of a mutually exclusive character, in essence things are not two but one.' World of life and death are aspects of the same thing, even so that there is no Nirvana except where there is Samsara (read, the cycle of birth, death and rebirth, so long as one lives in ignorance and does not know his own identity with Brahman), and no Samsara except where there is Nirvana.

Among multiple pointers emanating from the East in favour of non-duality, the following one suits our book here:

> To be and not to be arise mutually;
> Difficult and easy are mutually realized;
> Long and short are mutually contrasted;
> High and low are mutually posited;
> Before and after are in mutual sequence ...
> (Tao Te Ching)

32

# OUT OF BONDAGE

What follows does not lend itself to facile invocation or easy interpretation for that matter; yet for all intents and purposes it spells the hub of the whole issue, namely enlightenment or awakening. As has been submitted, the latter is a state of being and as such indescribable to suit ordinary language, yet not to the extent of mistaking the description of that state for that state itself! Enlightenment or awakening exists in the realm of direct, unmediated, 'de-polarized' experience whereby 'this' and 'that' are no longer separate entities, but different forms of the same thing: thus a manifestation of that which is beyond words, concepts, form, space and time. That which is, is, the wordless experience of that which is, we are told. In other parlance, enlightenment or awakening entails casting off all the bonds of concept (read more precisely, the veils of ignorance) in order to perceive directly, immediately the inexpressible nature of undifferentiated reality as the all-pervading unity of all things.

To illustrate the point, Izutsu[11] has it that 'the man of Zen aims at reducing all the historical forms of Buddhism to the enlightenment experience of the Buddha himself, re-experiencing it in its own original form, and plumbing the depths of spiritual life in a realm of the psyche which lies beyond the limits of the intellect.' To this end, one ought to methodically eliminate all intellection, since as long as the intellect remains activated, says Izutsu, one could never hope to

33

re-experience the original enlightenment of the Buddha. Moreover, 'this cannot be otherwise because what Zen considers to be the original experience of the Buddha is primarily an awakening to a dimension of supraconsciousness or an ontological awareness of Being in its pure 'suchness' prior to its being articulated into myriads of things and events through the discriminative activity of the intellect.'

There are at this stage enough pointers to further evidence, namely from Watts[13] to the effect that enlightenment or awakening in Zen parlance is living it, hence it cannot be fixed down to any form of words. It follows that the object of Zen is, as has been intimated earlier on, to go beyond words and ideas in order that the original insight of the Buddha be brought back to life. Another observation has it that Zen regards this insight as the one important thing, considering that 'scriptures are no more than devices, mere temporary expedients, for showing where it may be found.' Since it never makes the mistake of confusing teaching with wisdom, Zen is essentially that something 'which makes the difference between Buddha and an ordinary man.' Merton[4] enjoins upon saying that in Zen enlightenment the discovery of 'the original face before you were born' is the discovery, not that one 'sees' the Buddha, but that one 'is' Buddha and Buddha is not what the images of the temple had led one to expect: 'there is no longer any image, and consequently nothing to see, no one to see it, and a void in which no image is even conceivable.'

Speaking of awakening or enlightenment, let it be pointed out that, as generally acknowledged, *kensho* is reserved for initial awakening needing deepening, and the notion of *satori* reserved for those who, in the wake of Shakyamuni the Buddha, have attained Buddha-

34

hood, Zen Masters belonging to this class. Yet let it be borne in mind too that these two terms are not separable in that *kensho* moves, as it were, on to *satori* as one single ongoing process, the end product of which being illumination or, as Merton has it more succinctly, awakening of pure being beyond subject and object, or the resolution of all subject/object relationships and opposites in pure Void. Another version of *kensho* emanates from Humphreys[28] in that it is a 'first showing', an experience, if sustained, leads on to *satori*, yet not the goal of Zen; rather, the opening of the path to non-duality, or the first peep, the deeper experience as *satori* being the essential Zen experience. Nevertheless, 'the moment of *kensho* equates what we see, pour the heart and mind into the thing, the situation, until no seer no seen: only seeing.'

As has been noted, epistemologically speaking, *satori* for its part is the synthesis of affirmation and negation; psychologically speaking, overstepping the 'I'; metaphysically, discovering that being is becoming and becoming being. However, in terms that would beg the obvious, it could be asked what of the *satori* which has such a weighty significance in Zen as characterizing the whole trend of Japanese culture? Here is the answer provided by Suzuki[23], in that *satori* is generally translated as 'enlightenment', but 'awakening' may be a better term for it, bearing in mind that it is both noetic and affective. It is in fact 'to make opening to our most fundamental mental activity – the activity which has not differentiated itself into anything to be definitely called this or that.' What the author is telling us here is that when *satori* is experienced, 'something far more basic than either intellect or feeling is brought forward into the field of consciousness, though not in a relative sense.'

Now, the reason why 'awakening' is more appropriate than 'enlightenment' to describe the nature of *satori* is that 'while enlightenment is a static state of consciousness, awakening is a process which instantly brightens up the field of consciousness like a flash of lightning though it does not mean that the consciousness thus illuminated goes back to its former drabness.'

The clarity of Suzuki's exposé encourages the attempt to proceed further afield. Hence, being told by him elsewhere[2] that the enlightenment experience means going beyond the world of psychology, the opening of *prajna*-eye, and seeing into the realm of ultimate reality, notwithstanding landing on the other shore of Samsara where all things are viewed in their suchness or purity (read, *tathata* to be dealt with later on). On the other hand, attainment of Buddhahood means becoming thoroughly empty in the view of Zen Master Shosan Suzuki, hence meaning that one returns to the primordial state (read non-differentiation) in which there is not a speck of the 'I', the 'other', the Truth, even the Buddha, nothing remaining in one's mind, even the thought of enlightenment. This, incidentally, coheres with what our mentor[34] intimates, that is, enlightenment as beyond every mode of expression, beyond all thought-construction created by the mind, and whose characterization is transferable by *prajna* of which it can be said that it is seeing into the essence of things as they are (more about this further on).

Perhaps another explanation about enlightenment might be useful here, hence Conrad Hyers'[19] to the effect that, Zen being beyond striving and seeking, true awakening entails a liberation intended to flow forth and spontaneously, notwithstanding an immediacy that precludes the distinction between what is sought for and the act of seeking for it. In effect, as long as one is seeking, one does not realize one's possession of the Buddha nature that is anticipatory to one's seeking, and the precondition for it. The author goes on to say that as in the case one is endowed with one's Buddha nature (read, in the true and original sense), one doesn't really need to seek for it; rather, 'be it'.

In this connection, our attention is drawn once again to Izutsu[11] on the grounds that the realization of Self-nature or Buddha-nature is nothing other than the attainment of Buddha-hood. In more specific terms, Self-nature is the noumenon as the ultimate ground of all phenomena. It is, says he, the metaphysical depth of Being itself, the unity of all things (read, not in the sense of unification, but as primordial non-differentiation), the Ground of all things before it is bifurcated into the ego-entity of the objective world.

The insights gained thus far find, so to speak, their natural outlet among some of the Zen Masters of ancient China whose views on enlightenment ran as follows[35]:

'Delusion means you are not aware of your own fundamental mind; enlightenment means you realize your own fundamental essence. Once enlightened you do not become deluded any more.' (Zen Master Mazu)

'The pure light in a moment of awareness in your mind is the Buddha's essence within you. The non-discriminative light in a moment of awareness in your mind is the Buddha's wisdom in you. The undifferentiated light in a moment of awareness in your mind is the Buddha's manifestation in you.' (Zen Master Linji)

'I explain to you matters pertaining to enlightenment, but don't try to keep your mind on them.

37

Just turn to the ocean of your essence and develop practical accord with its true nature.' (Zen Master Yangshan)

'When you are settled in Zen, your mind is serene, unaffected by distractions. You enter the realm of enlightenment, and transcend the ordinary world, leaving the world while in the midst of society.' (Zen Master Fenyang)

'Enlightenment is experienced instantaneously, but Zen work must be done over a long time, like a bird that when first hatched is naked and scrawny, but then grows feathers as it is nourished, until it can fly high and far.' (Zen Master Yan-wu)

'Buddhas and Zen Masters do not have different realization; they all reach a point of cessation, where past, present and future are cut off and all impulses stop, where there is not the slightest object. Enlightened awareness shines spontaneously, subtly penetrating the root source.' (Zen Master Hongzhi)

In search of a personal understanding of the issue, it runs into something like this[29]:

> Banking on awakening alone
> Would be way off the mark;
> Talking about it,
> Missing the whole point.
> Neither banking nor talking,
> Once one's true nature unfolded
> Along the 'pathless path',
> Or through the 'gateless gate',
> Just looking at things
> In their eternal Suchness.

At this stage, it calls for coping, this time, with enlightenment or awakening epistemologically and ontologically speaking. Calling on Izutsu[36], we are told that the initial stage of awakening embodies mind, perception and sensation relating to the articulated and differentiated forms of reality, or multiplicity/diversity belonging to the external world. In Zen parlance, the mountain is the mountain. This initial stage is followed by a transitional period during which the mind enters meditation properly speaking, that is, it starts gradually to lose consciousness of the external world concomitantly with the gradual obliteration of ego-consciousness.

The second or pre-awakening stage is characterized by a state of pure consciousness beyond the dichotomy subject/object, that is, opposed to the ordinary consciousness of something. There ensues no trace of the 'I' as subject of cognizance in that the subject/object split of reality is obliterated. This is the realm of *wu-hsin* or *mushin* (No-Mindedness) as spiritual dimension of Being beyond space-time. As has been the case with the previous stage, the pre-awakening stage is followed by another transitional period during which the actual realization of awakening begins to take place, that is, *kensho* leading eventually to *satori*. It means that the mind, leaving behind the state of pure consciousness, is called upon to revert to the state of ordinary consciousness-of-something, that is, by gradually reinstating the subject/object cognition yet within, this time, an internally transformed or illuminated consciousness. In Zen parlance, the mountain is no more the mountain.

The third stage of awakening spells a total difference with the initial stage in that, whereas the mountain is once again the mountain, all things in the world are seen as, and identified with, the many forms of the non-articulated; as the manifested form of the non-manifested; as the many within the one. All things and everything are looked upon from the vantage point of self-articulated of the non-articulated, the self-mani-festing activity of the non-manifested, the multiple within unity. A most lucid or intuitive thing, that is, a stage of oneness with the All.

Viewed as a metaphysical process, the gradual merging of the initial stage means that the phenomenal or external world of multiplicity within its infinite diversity, is being gradually reduced to a state of unity whereby things lose their ontological difference. They become submerged in an absolute non-articulation and non-differentiation equating utter plenitude of Being, a state of ultimate Source-Ground or *sunyata* (Emptiness or Void). Phenomena are, as it were, recovered after having been 'lost', that is, they are significantly different from what they were before in that, by now, all of them are 'open' and no more 'closed'. In other words, all things are ontologically transparent and seen in their Suchness (*tathata*), yet paradoxically articulated and differentiated while non-articulated and non-differentiated at the same time. They interpenetrate each other and 'fuse' into one another within a sort of ontological fluidity.

In summation, with the initial stage, pre-awakening and awakening relating to enlightenment, we have a three-in-one process as follows.

| Initial Stage | Pre-Awakening | Awakening |
| --- | --- | --- |
| Mind<br>Ego or 'I' | *Wu-hsin* or *mushin* (No-Mindedness). Gradual elimination of the Ego or 'I'. Complete release from it (*anatta*) | *Kensho* or initial awakening needing deepening until *satori* is attained, or one's Buddha nature achieved |
| Duality of subject and object, body and mind. Phenomenal world in its concreteness | Neither subject nor object as such. Unity of opposites | Subject and object once more evident. Both united prior to their bifurcation |
| Being and non-being within their diversity and multiplicity | Neither being nor non-being. Things without their ontological difference | Being and non-being once again. Experience of *tathata* (Suchness) at hand |
| Externalization: 'The mountain is the mountain' | 'The mountain is no more the mountain' | 'The mountain is once more the mountain'. Unity of body and mind within the All. Integrative vision |

End point: awareness of Being beyond relationship of subject object in pure Void (*sunyata* = *prajna*)

Judging from the above, the outstanding pivotal elements in need of further elaboration comprise unity of opposites, *prajna*, *sunyata* and *tathata* following suit.

# UNITY OF THE OPPOSITES

One of the most powerful motivations is the need we feel to make sense of our experiences, to gain a coherent and satisfying understanding of the world in which we live, writes John Polkinghorne[37]. This being the case, we take it that the notion of the opposites come into it, a notion which, as is well known, goes back to Classical Greece with Heraclitus of Ephesus (c.550–480 BCE). Nicknamed 'the Obscure' or 'the Riddler', the famed philosopher pointed out that the world is characterized by opposites, that is, without this dynamic play of opposites the world couldn't exist. Moreover, such a dynamic play of opposites or contraries is due to what contains and transcends them at the same time, that is, the Logos or higher principle taken as the rational principle governing the cosmos and which, as oneness, implies the source of all things. However, a note of warning at this stage from Watts[38] in that at the very roots of Chinese thinking and feeling there lies the principle of polarity which is not to be confused with the ideas of opposition or conflict. In effect, says he, 'in the metaphor of other cultures, light is at war with darkness, life with death, good with evil, and the positive with the negative.' Hence, an idealism to cultivate the former and be rid of the latter flourishes in our midst.

What can be assumed, though, is that the Heraclitean Logos bears a somewhat striking analogy with the Tao ('dow') of Lao-tzu (sixth–fifth century BCE) as the

Primal Meaning of Undivided Unity in the words of F. C. Happold[39]. On the other hand, the Logos as higher principle containing and transcending the opposites, coheres with the similar thesis submitted some two centuries later by Chuang-tzu (c.369–286). In other words, the Logos, as a process arising from the interplay of the opposites, is a key concept which subsumes that, as has been observed, insight ought to interpret evidence and wisdom lies in intuiting the unity behind the diversity of all things.

This brings us to a further piece of evidence in that, as major aspect of reality, the Logos anticipates by some ten centuries the key to Nicolas of Cusa's thought (alias Nicklaus von Kues, 1401–91), namely his *Coincidentia Oppositorum*, notwithstanding much later on C. G. Jung's Unity Principle, and Niels Bohr's Principle of Complementarity in quantum physics.

The whole issue is given wider scope by Ken Wilber[40] in that the root of the whole difficulty is 'our tendency to view opposites as irreconcilable, as totally set apart and divorced from one another'. The point is that the opposites share an implicit identity; they remain completely inseparable and mutually interdependent (read, one simply could not exist without the other). Now, pursues the author, the unity of opposites is hardly confined to mystics, East and West, and 'if one looks to modern-day physics, the field in which Western intellect has made its greatest advance, what we find is another version of reality as a union of the opposites.'

Speaking of modern physics, one of its well-known representatives, Wolfgang Pauli[41], has argued that we Westerners must acknowledge the opposites to be complementary. Moreover, contrary to the strict division of the human spirit into separate departments which has prevailed since the nineteenth century onwards, Pauli advocates the overcoming of the opposites. While the author endorses such a fundamental view, including the synthesis embracing both rational understanding and the mystical experience of unity, the trouble lies in our Western habits of primarily seeing and thinking of everything in terms of opposites and, by the same token, failing to recognize the commonality and unity that underlie them, suggests Roger Walsh[42].

As so it goes on and on, because, as Humphreys[28] has it, we are bound by fetters of thought in a world of opposites, and so far as mind is concerned we 'know' nothing save by a compound of choices between them. In other parlance, all description of things, visible and invisible, is achieved by a build-up of selected terms for untold pairs of opposites. In the end, 'we are still in the dual field of the opposites, and we still do not "know": we only "know" about, though it may be a great deal about it.' The author tells us elsewhere[12] that the point is not to regard the opposites as parallel lines which can never meet, rather, we would imagine, acknowledging the central role of the Logos containing and transcending them at the same time.

The foregoing having been taken care of, our next task is to address ourselves to the trans-cultural, trans-religious and transformed elements of consciousness, namely, *prajna*, *sunyata* (Emptiness or Void) and *tathata* (Suchness).

# A SPECIAL INTUITION WITHOUT OBJECT

What is proposed here is conceivable at the most profound level of insight, namely, *prajna* as transcendental wisdom getting hold, writes Suzuki[43], of wholeness and individuality of things in one go. It is an unmediated intuition as the result of direct, immediate perception. Put in a nutshell, *prajna* is reality epistemologically speaking; psychologically stated, it is the most fundamental experience beyond the differentiation of subject/object; metaphysically expressed, it is the awakening of *sunyata* to self-consciousness. As such it can be said that *prajna* is the ultimate reality itself, or *sunyata* is *prajna*, and that *prajna*-eye or *prajna*-intuition is becoming conscious of itself.

At this point, let it be made clear that the seeing in question is not just ordinary seeing by means of relative knowledge, but the seeing by means of *prajna*-eye tantamount to a kind of special intuition enabling us to penetrate right into the bedrock of reality itself, says Suzuki. In other words, *prajna* can be taken as a special intuition distinct from the current type of intuition philosophically and religiously speaking in that it is without object, without a state of identification between subject and object, hence transcendental in nature (read, it is never 'this' or 'that').

It could be inferred too that *prajna* is pure act, pure experience; it is comparable to a flash of lightning, hence meaning immediacy, no deliberation, no allowance for any intervening proposition, no passing from premise to conclusion. Our mentor has it next that *prajna* is actively itself, not mere activity-feeling. It is not object, it is activity itself, its own creator out of its own free will. When *prajna*-intuition takes place, as it were, the space-time relationship is annihilated, and all existence reduced to a point-instant, hence its fundamental noetic principle as the essence of Buddhist philosophy whereby a synthetic apprehension of the whole is possible.

Suzuki's exposé goes the right way towards summing up the issue as follows[34]: '*Prajna* is grasping the ungraspable, attaining the unattainable, comprehending the incomprehensible; that when this intellectual description of the working of *prajna* is translated into psychological terms, it is not becoming attached to anything, whether it is an idea or feeling.'

*Prajna* being such a core notion toward the appreciation of Zen, it is worthwhile going into another fundamental version of it submitted, this time, by Merton[10]. Hence, *prajna* does not consist in abiding in a secret mystical point in one's being, but abiding nowhere in particular, 'neither in self or out of self. It does not consist in self-realization as an affirmation of one's own limited being, or as a fruition of one's inner spiritual essence, but on the contrary, it is liberated from the need of self-affirmation and self-realization whatever.' Merton goes on to say that *prajna* as a word is not self-realization, but realization pure and simple, beyond subject and object. Moreover 'in self-realization, evidently "emptiness" is not opposed to "fullness", but emptiness and fullness are One. Zero equals infinity.' Otherwise stated, the definite moment of *prajna* is insight into the nature of reality, a realization incidentally Zen equates with the attainment of Buddhahood.

Rounding the issue, here are some excerpts from the *Sutra* of Hui-neng (Wei-lang; Jap: Eno) on *prajna*[44]:

'Learned audience, those who recite the word Prajna the whole day long do not seem to know that Prajna is inherent in their nature. But mere talking of food will not appease hunger, and this is exactly the case with these people...'

'Learned audience, what is Prajna? It means Wisdom ... one foolish notion is enough to shut off Prajna, while one wise thought will bring it forth again ... the Heart of Wisdom is Prajna, which has neither form nor characteristic...'

'Learned audience, to use Prajna for contemplation, and to take an attitude of neither indifference nor attachment towards all things – this is what is meant by realizing one's own Essence of Mind for the attainment of Buddhahood...'

'Learned audience ... Prajna does not vary with different persons; what makes the difference is whether one's mind is enlightened or deluded...'

# AN ALL-INCLUSIVE MYSTERY

A wide discernment surrounds the notion of *sunyata* (Emptiness or Void; Ch: *ku'ung*: Jap: *ku*) as basic tenet of both Taoism and Mahayana Buddhism, hence warranting extensive examination here. Issued from the Madhyamika school of the Mahayana, regarded as the pinnacle of Buddhist philosophy, with its founder Nagarjuna (c.100–200), himself probably the most influential among Mahayana philosophers. As Wilber[45] has it, Nagarjuna was the finest great sage to not only see but fully enunciate in dialectic fashion the 'Dharmakaya-Void', 'thus drawing out and extending on the Buddha's original insight.' The gist of Nagarjuna's philosophy, though, is to have demonstrated that ultimate reality cannot be grasped intellectually, hence his notion of *sunyata* as being independently real.

Unfortunately, enjoins philosopher Chandradhar Sharma[46], the word '*sunyata*' has been gravely misunderstood, and its literal meaning, which is negation or void, has been the cause of that misunderstanding. In effect, ignoring the real philosophical meaning of the word '*sunyata*' and taking it only in the literal sense, many thinkers, Eastern and Western alike, ancient, medieval and modern, have unfortunately 'committed that blunder which has led them to thoroughly misunderstand *sunyata* and to condemn it as hopeless scepticism and self-condemned nihilism.' In fact, pursues Sharma, according to the Madhyamika *sunyata* does not mean 'nothing' or an empty void or 'negative

48

abyss', but essentially means Indescribable; it is Reality which ultimately transcends existence, non-existence, both and neither.

Woven around the same theme, we hear from Suzuki next[43] that the doctrine of *sunyata* is one of the best-known ones, yet one of the least understood, especially by those unfamiliar with Mahayana ontology, 'not even comprehended by some Buddhist scholars'. The reason given is that, owing to its subtlety of depth, or its supreme simplicity for that matter, the doctrine itself is apt to be wrongly or inadequately interpreted. The author goes on to say that, as a doctrine, *sunyata* is not the absolute annihilation but the denial of a relative world or world of appearance as final reality where birth and death occur. According to the Mahayana, that world of form-and-name and the inner world of thought and feeling are no more than the construction of mind, and when the latter ceases through *wu-hsin* or *mushin* (No-Mindness) the weaving out of the world of particulars ceases, this ceasing being called Void or Emptiness, explains Suzuki.

In summation, *sunyata* does not deny the external world, the world of multiplicities, in that 'mountains are there, the cherries in full bloom, the moon shines brightly in the autumnal night, but at the same time they are no more than peculiarities, they are understood in relation to what they are not.' An additional remark has it that Zen emptiness is not emptiness or nothingness, but the emptiness of fullness in which there is 'no gain, no loss, no increase, no decrease, in which the equation zero equals infinity takes place'. Elsewhere[27], we hear that, as one of the most important notions in Mahayana philosophy, *sunyata* is at the same time the most puzzling for non-Buddhist readers to comprehend. When Buddhists declare all things to be empty, 'they are not advocating a nihilistic view; on the contrary an ultimate reality is hinted at, which cannot be subsumed under the categories of logic.'

Lama Anagarika Govinda[47] sets out his own version to the effect that *sunyata* as concept is not a negative one at all, since it means 'the creative void out of which everything comes into existence, not incidentally, without a close parallel with contemporary physics.' For his part, Wilber[39] has good reason to believe that *sunyata* is void of thought because the latter is that which as 'our symbolic map-making' is the very process which superimposes boundaries on reality. Hence when Zen says that reality is void, it means that it is void of boundaries. Another view emanates from philosopher Renée Weber[47] when she argues that *sunyata* denotes the unconditioned, that is, the original, unbroken ground of being about which we can only speak in terms of symbols. Yet, intuited by experience, it is a state of undifferentiated unity beyond subject and object distinction and beyond space and time.

It makes sense at this stage to be reminded by Watts[48] that for the Mahayana *sunyata* is the highest tate of spiritual consciousness in which one apprehends ultimate reality (read, Dharmakaya-Void) in a direct, unmediated manner, considering that the Buddhist principle that form is void doesn't mean that there are no forms, rather that the latter are inseparable from their context. There are thus no self-evident forms, since the 'more one concentrates upon the individual thing, the more it turns out to involve the whole universe.'

When it comes to Bede Griffiths next[49], he submits that all phenomenal reality comes forth from the void, hence *sunyata* boasting of a twin aspect: immanent and transcendent. Immanent in the whole universe and along with this is the profound idea of the interrelatedness of all phenomena, this, incidentally going back to the Buddha's early teaching which stressed that all phenomena are interrelated and dynamic rather than static forms of interrelationship. *Sunyata* is also transcendent, for it is the absolute, beyond thought, beyond the senses, beyond all phenomena. Now, in Nagarjuna's understanding, says Griffiths, the universe viewed as a whole is the Absolute, while viewed as process is the phenomenal world.

Reverting to Watts[13] for a moment, he points out that Nagarjuna's celebrated Doctrine of the Void refutes all metaphysical propositions by demonstrating their relativity. Otherwise stated, Nagarjuna's method is simply to show that all things are without self-nature (read, *svabbava*) or independent reality since they exist only in relation to other things. Nothing in the universe can stand by itself – no thing, no being, no event, and for this reason, says he, it is absurd to single anything out as the ideal to be grasped. 'For what is singled out exists only in relation to its opposite, since that it is defined by what is not.' Little wonder, then, that *sunyata* has been called the all-inclusive mystery in that, as Humphreys[28] points out, it implies that behind all things is No-thing, which is not nothing but that which precedes all things and all thing-ness. Its essential nature cannot be defined.

As a final touch, this time from a Taoist source, the notion of Void or Emptiness is given one of its finest expressions by Chuang-tzu here:[50]

In the beginning was the Void, the Nameless.
And in the Nameless was the One, without body,
  without form
This one – this Being in whom all find power
  to exist

Is the Living.
From the living comes the Formless, the Undivided.
From the act of this Formless come the Existents,
each according
To its inner principle. This is Form. Here body
 embraces
and cherishes spirit.
The two work together as one, bending and
 manifesting
their Characters. And this is Nature.

# THE ESSENCE OF ALL THINGS ALIKE

Another vista on our understanding of the issue, albeit without a metaphysical axe to grind, concerns *tathata* or Suchness of all things which, closely linked to the fundamental notion of *sunyata* (Emptiness or Void) points, in keeping with Buddhist philosophy, at seeing reality as it is. As doctrine, it comes from Indian thinker and sage Ashvaghosha (second century CE), notwithstanding that it became later on very prominent in Zen. More details are supplied by Ernest Wood[24] in that *tathata*, literally 'That-way-ness' is usually translated as 'suchness' as the essential description of what a thing is, 'but it is non-descriptive in that it does not compare the thing with anything else,' but simply refers to the thing, saying in effect that 'it is', quite different from anything else. Another observation has it that emptiness is suchness and suchness emptiness, because the suchness of anything is devoid of any other thing; and again, it is *prajna* that realizes suchness to the same extent that it denotes the void, self-nature.

At this stage, it is noteworthy that for Edward Conze *tathata* or Suchness is the central notion of the Mahayana referring to the absolute, the true nature of all things, immutable, immovable, and beyond all concepts and distinctions; in fact, the very opposite of phenomena. *Tathata* or Suchness, writes Sharma[46], is Reality; as harmonious whole, *dharmakaya*, or *dharmadhatu* (read, reality beyond being and non-being); as the ultimate existence, Nirvana or breaking through the cycle of life and death. Sharma comes to the conclusion that *tathata* or Suchness is not encompassable by the intellect, and hence essentially in-describable; it is neither unity nor plurality nor both nor neither; it is neither existence nor non-existence nor both nor neither.

As unitive apprehension, *tathata*, in the view of Aldous Huxley, is the ultimate ground which can be indicated, never described in verbal symbols; or the Ultimate or nature of all natures, the Absolute sewn through the fabric of all, that is, after Wilbur; or the 'be-ness' of everything, an ultimate spiritual essence beyond the opposites which condition human perception intimated by Happold. Interestingly enough, the 'be-ness' in question is akin to the 'is-ness' (*isticheit*) of Meister Eckhart, the Rhenan mystic (1260–1328).

It would be appropriate to listen now to what Suzuki[22] has to tell us about *tathata* or Suchness. To begin with, it is a philosophical term, and when of religious import, it is called *dharmakaya*, the latter, incidentally, does not exactly express all the ideas it contains. Suchness is neither that which is existent, nor that which is non-existent. In short, it is neither that which is at once existent and non-existent; it is altogether beyond the conception of the human intellect, and the best way of designating it seems to call it Suchness.

Hyers[19] brings more purchase to the argument upon remarking that by way of Suchness things are seen perfectly clearly 'beyond the filter of categories and in an usually fresh and lucid light'. On the other hand, this suchness of things 'is a perception of their inexhaustible mystery ... in the sense of an ultimate mystery that it is to be found in even the most obvious and ordinary area of experience where no particular problem appears at all, and where no absurdity is immediately apparent.'

While we are at it we may as well be reminded by Humphreys that Suchness is non-temporal, non-spatial, non-dual reality, and, as last pointer, we may quote two verses from the mystical poem of Seng-ts'an (Sosan Zenji in Japanese, third Patriarch of Zen in China, c.600, which to our mind characterize the spirit of *tathata* or Suchness best, albeit not without their share of paradox, as couched in the non-dualistic language of the times[51]:

When the deep mystery of Suchness is fathomed,
All of a sudden we forget the external entanglements;
When the ten thousand things are viewed in their
   oneness,
We return to the origin and remain where we have
   always been ...

In the higher realm of Suchness
There is neither 'self' or 'other';
When direct identification is sought,
We can only say 'not two' ...

# THE TOUCHSTONE IS EXPERIENCE

As a spin-off of what has been articulated thus far, there remains in the balance the experience of Zen itself as a proposition of choice, so much so that it has encouraged Humphreys[28] to intimate that such an experience at the heart of Zen is beyond duality, and therefore beyond the range and reach of the highest thinking owing to the fact that Zen is because there is Nothing – No-thing in it: Zen is Zen because it has left the intellect well behind. Merton[10] steps in upon remarking that in contrast to our Western elaborate philosophical and theological formulations, Buddhist metaphysics is hardly doctrinal, rather basically simple, as natural elaboration of the implications of the Buddha's own enlightenment. 'Buddhism does not primarily seek to understand or to "believe" in the enlightenment of the Buddha as the solution of all problems, but seeks an existential experience.' In other parlance, Zen gets back, as far as possible, to the pure inarticulated and unexplained ground of direct experience of Life itself: the naked reality of experience is grasped as the awareness of the ontological ground of our being here and now, right in the midst of the world.

We would furthermore agree with Powell[16] when he submits that the essential thing to realize is that in the final analysis it is only the Zen experience that counts: 'the approach and the experience are still worlds apart'. That is, the former is confined within the limits of conceptual thinking (read, and as such liable to arguments, to opinion), while the experience itself is beyond the level of concepts and independent of space and time, says he.

Our understanding of the issue is further enhanced upon being told by Suzuki[52] that Zen experience is complete only when it is backed up by Zen consciousness. In fact, Zen expects us to experience within ourselves that the Suchness of things (*tathata*) is beyond the ken of intellectual pointing and dialectical process, no amount of words can succeed in describing it. The real trouble, though, is that whenever we try to talk about things beyond intellection is that we always make our start from intellection itself. It follows that when, for instance, Zen experience is talked about it sounds empty, as if possessing no positive value. But 'Zen proposes that we effect a complete *volte-face* and make our stance first on Zen experience itself and then observe things (read, the world of being and non-being) from the point of view of the experience itself'.

The foregoing calls for further elaboration in that, reverting to Powell, it is unfortunately not possible to 'teach' anybody to have the Zen experience, three major obstacles standing in the way of that experience, particularly for us in the West. To begin with, there is the general idea of gain in people's minds as when on first hearing of Zen they immediately ask: 'What do I get out of it?' The second obstacle is this: the tendency for people to question everything according to a moral yardstick added to the desire for facile classification when actually based on an undercurrent of righteousness. Finally, there is our Catesian heritage seen as a malady by the East, to the extent that we are suffering from a sort of schizophrenia.

As a leading proponent of Zen in the West acknowledged by many, including the present writer, it is little wonder to be told by Merton[4] that the convenient tools of language enable us to 'decide beforehand what we think things mean, and tempt us all too easily to see things only in a specific way that fits our logical preoccupations and our verbal formulas.' In other parlance, instead of seeing things and facts as they are we see them as reflections and verifications of the sentences we have previously made up in our minds. At the limit, 'we quickly forget how to simply see things ... so that we see only what conveniently fits our prejudices.'

This extends to another piece of evidence submitted, this time, by writer George Steiner[53] to the effect that, referring to the highest, purest reach of the contemplative act, it is that which has learned to leave language behind it. This, incidentally, is not without analogy to Zen experience as the ineffable which lies beyond the frontiers of the world in the course of meditation. When such understanding is attained, pursues the author, the evidence needs no longer 'suffer the impurities and fragmentation that speech entails. It need not conform to the naive logic and linear conception of time implicit in syntax.'

To put the matter in a broader perspective, we are by now in a better position to appreciate how much the experience of Zen stems from a gradual insight notably through meditation, that is, to the extent that it cannot be communicated in any kind of doctrinal formula or even any precise phenomenological description. The experience of Zen strictly speaking lies beyond a system of pantheistic monism, or of a system of any kind for that matter; neither does it fit into mysticism of withdrawal nor ascesis; neither into a religious or lay formulation. In fact, the experience of Zen is alien to any philosophical or psychological perspective, nor does it embody quietistic inaction nor the suppression of the thinking process. In fact, it is, as acknowledged, a breakthrough, an explosive liberation and a recovery of unity which is not the suppression of the opposites but an utter simplicity beyond the opposites as Merton intimates.

Having inferred that the experience of Zen doesn't present clear and definitely recognizable characteristics capable of being set down in words, the outcome, as we have already seen, is a direct grasp of one's true, original or Buddha nature through arriving at mind by having no mind (*wu-hsin* or *mushin*); better still, 'being' mind instead of 'having' no mind as Merton has it. The result is at once a liberation from the delusion of ego-centeredness (*anatta*), not a withdrawal within one's spiritual essence and a denial of matter and of the world. On the contrary, 'the Zen experience is a recognition that the whole world is aware of itself in us.'

# THE INSTANTANEOUS QUALITY

With his customary insight blessed with erudition, Suzuki[9] can well afford to state that 'when the mind now abiding in its isness (read, is free from intellectual complexities and moralistic attachments of every kind) surveys the world of the senses in all multiplicities, it discovers in it all sorts of values hitherto hidden from sight. Here opens to the artist a world full of wonders and miracles.' It follows that the artist's world is one of free creation, and this can come 'only from intuitions directly and immediately arising from the isness of things, unhampered by senses and intellect.' The artist creates from forms and sounds out of formlessness and soundlessness, to the extent, though, that the world of the artist coincides with that of Zen.

Speaking of aesthetics, Watts[13] points out that since 'one showing is worth a hundred sayings', the expression of Zen in the arts gives us one of the most direct ways of understanding it. This is the more so because the art forms created by Zen are not symbolic in nature, the favourite subjects of Zen artists are natural, concrete, and secular things, that is, depicted in a peculiar down-to-earth and human way. Moreover, the world of art is considered not only as representing nature but by being itself a work of nature according to the author.

When it comes to the influence of Zen as reflected in Japanese art and culture, Watts tells us elsewhere[54] that three major characteristics pave the way to a better understanding of Zen art. To begin with, absence of symmetry in that the phenomena of nature are rarely symmetrical in form; at most, only an approximation to absolute symmetry, and Zen 'perceives in this fact the lively and dynamic quality of nature.' In effect, 'symmetry is a state of such perfect balance that movement is no longer possible; a form so balanced is dead, and thus the symmetrical form is analogous to that mental and emotional fixation which in Zen is broken down.'

The second characteristic is the use of emptiness in that Zen deplores the cluttering of a picture or of a room with many objects. Like the Chinese paintings, it makes the greater use of empty backgrounds, of large expanses of mist to suggest depth, while bearing in mind the empty spaces are no mere emptiness: they are creative and suggestive, 'exciting the imagination and giving startling clarity and vividness to the objects against and within them.' Finally, the instantaneous quality which might be called, too, the momentary quality, for 'Chinese and Japanese art love to portray moments of life, as if the painter had just glimpsed his subject for a second.' Besides, the very media of the art – brush, ink or silk or absorbent paper – require a swift, evenly flowing technique in that, as well-known as life itself, a stroke once made can never be retouched.

One would readily agree with Humphreys when he submits that with Zen it is a matter of another aesthetic discipline in which first comes the technique so mastered that it is forgotten; then the use of it. Now, although we have addressed the issue elsewhere[29] we are appealing once again to Suzuki[9], who reminds us that in the realm of painting, the true aesthetic ascetism is characterized by asymmetry, imbalance, the 'one-corner' style, plus the notions of *wabi* and *sabi*.

*Wabi* is psychologically associated with the Japanese painters' thrifty brush tradition whereby the least possible number of brush strokes, a way of sheer economy representing forms on paper or silk, are retained. Another version thereof has it as the transcendent aloofness in the midst of simplicity, poverty in the sense of not being dependent on current fashion, fame, social status, and so forth: the inward, timeless feeling of something of the highest value. *Wabi*, pursues the author, literally means 'solitariness' and, more to the point, 'poverty'. It is, as it were, what characterizes the whole Japanese culture endowed with the spirit of Zen. The expression poverty is, incidentally, meant in both economic and spiritual sense. Zen inclines to poverty, free from the idea of position; Zen is poverty.

Suzuki has another point upon suggesting that both 'one-corner' style and *wabi* break through human art artificially, taking hold, so to speak, of a sense of imperfection becoming perfection of form. When this beauty of imperfection is accompanied by primitive uncouthness, we have a glimpse of *sabi*, so prized by Japanese connoisseurs. We are dealing here with a rustic unpretentiousness, an apparent simplicity or effortlessness in execution, and possibly richness in historical association, notwithstanding an inexplicable element that is part and parcel of artistic achievement.

Another notion of Japanese art coming to the fore is *myopa* or *daoyu*, or simply *myo*, whereby the relationship of things ceases to be valued, that is, as Suzuki explains, something 'defying the challenge of man's thinking power; a mode of activity which comes directly out of one's innermost self without being intercepted by the dichotomous intellect.' The act is so direct and immediate that 'intellection finds no room here to insert itself and cut it to pieces.' In other parlance, *myo* is 'a certain artistic quality perceptible not only in works of art, but in anything in Nature and life.'

To get the full meaning of the situation one has to get acquainted with the fact that, from a Zen viewpoint, mere technical knowledge of art is not enough to make man really the master of his craft, unless he has delved deeply into the inner spirit of it all, pursues Suzuki. However, this spirit is graspable provided the artist is in complete harmony with the principle of life itself, that is, when he has attained to a state we have already come across, namely, *wu-hsin* or *mushin* (No-mindness), a state beyond dualism of all forms of being and non-being. This is where all arts merge into Zen, No-mindness in this particular instance being regarded as a state that 'gives itself up to an unknown power that comes from nowhere and yet seems strong enough to possess the whole field of consciousness and makes it work from the unknown.'

For example, if one draws a bamboo, it means that one is being called upon to 'become' a bamboo and forget that one is one while drawing it. This is thus the Zen of the bamboo, this is the moment with 'the rhythmic movement of the spirit' residing in both the bamboo and the artist himself, upon the understanding, though, that the artist has a firm hold on the spirit of it all and yet conscious of it. This, incidentally, is the task achieved after a long spiritual training, a difficult discipline to which, since earliest times, Eastern artists have been taught to subject themselves, remarks the author.

With calligraphy art to be considered next, Rawson and Legeza[55] introduce another element of discussion in that the hand of the calligrapher, prompted by the momentary intuition of inner spirit, does execute a vivid dance across the rice paper or silk, and in this dance the traces left by the gesture convey their own extra meaning or 'meaning beyond text'. Moreover, each linked group of strokes becomes an expression of kinetic trace which has never been written before, and never will again; otherwise stated, 'the meaning beyond the text as resonance evoked by traces, each one being unique'.

Closest to the feeling of Zen, enjoins Watts[13], is the calligraphy style involving the touch of the brush, light and fluid, and since it must move continuously over the absorbent paper, 'if the ink is to flow regularly its control requires a free movement of the hand and arm as if one were dancing rather than writing on paper.' Equally impressive is the mastery of the brush, of strokes ranging from delicate elegance to rough vitality. In other words, this technique, known as *zenga* style, has been preserved even in painting from minutely detailed trees to bold outlines and masses given 'texture by the controlled accidents of stray brush hairs and uneven inking on paper.'

Our interest is conducive to a different topic, namely that of *haiku* or the 17-syllable Japanese poem as, moreover, the shortest form of poem in the world literature and which, in the words of R.H. Blyth, 'is the experience of a temporary enlightenment in which we see into the life of things.' To revert to Watts, the non-Japanese listener must remember that a good *haiku* 'is a pebble thrown into the pool of the listener's mind, evoking association out of the richness of his own memory. It invites the listener to participate instead of leaving him dumb with admiration while the poet shows off.'

Stepping in once again, Suzuki points out that while the shortness of the *haiku* has, incidentally, nothing to do with the significance of the content, and whether temporary or not, 'the author of the *haiku* gives it a significant intuition of Reality.' In brief, the *haiku* ought to be 'an expression of one's inner feeling altogether devoid of the sense of the ego.' For example, with the famous poem of Matsuo Basho (1643–94), to whom the development of the *haiku* was, incidentally, largely due

> The old pond, ah!
> A frog jumps in:
> The water's sound!

we are offered a deeper insight by Suzuki when he suggests that Basho discovered the suchness of things (*tathata*), that is, right in the sound of water the moment the frog jumped into the pond. In other words, the sound coming out of the pond was heard by the poet in no ordinary or pedestrian manner: it was a sound filling the whole universe. Moreover, not only was the totality of the environment absorbed in the sound and vanished into it, adds Suzuki, but Basho himself was altogether effaced from his consciousness (read, both subject and object, *en soi et pour soi*, ceased to be something confronting and conditioning each other). Lest the reader be perplexed at this stage, this could not be a state of complete annihilation in that, as Suzuki emphasizes, the poet was there, the old pond was there, with all the rest.

The message is clear from Basho's *haiku*: the poet was enlightened, that is, he underwent the experience of *satori* or full awakening upon hearing the sound of the water as the frog jumped into the old pond. Incidentally, such episodes of sudden illumination akin to a flash of lightning, are fairly frequent through Zen literature relating to the Rinzai school, as opposed to the gradual illumination proved by the Soto school. A last word about *haiku* is that, as Suzuki has indicated, this form of poem and Zen are not to be confused in that the former has its own field; it is poetry, but it also partakes of something of Zen, namely, at the point where one and the other get related.

The next item on our agenda is one which, in the words of Watts, has exercised an incalculable influence on Japanese culture imbued with the spirit of Zen: the Art of Tea Ceremony or *cha-no-yu* requiring, if necessary, no further apparatus than a bowl, tea, and hot water, although in the appropriate atmosphere. In fact, the monastic tea ceremony was introduced into Japan by Eisai Zenji (1141–1215), upon the understanding that its form is different from the present-day *cha-no-yu*, the latter having been perfected by Sen-no-Rikyu (1518–91). However, the spirit of Zen and the Tea Ceremony, says Suzuki[9], have in common the constant attempt at simplification, by which is meant elimination of the unnecessary achieved by Zen in its grasp of final reality.

To begin with, *cha-no-yu* is the way of living typified by serving tea in the appropriate tea-room; it is the aestheticism of primitive simplicity. Moreover, such an art is intimately connected with Zen not only in its practical development but principally in the observance of the spirit that runs through the ceremony itself. In other parlance, such a spirit in terms of feeling consists of harmony (*wa*) or gentleness (*garawagi*), reverence (*kei*), purity (*sei*), and tranquillity (*jaku*). Here are the four elements needed for bringing the Tea Ceremony to fruition, as well as providing the essential constituents to a brotherly and orderly life akin to the one met in a Zen monastery.

66

Now, pursues Suzuki, the first two elements, *wa* or *garawagi* and *kei* are social and ethical; the third one, *sei*, both physical and psychological; the fourth one, *jaku*, spiritual and metaphysical. Finally, the spirit of the Tea Ceremony is deeply seeped in the *prajna* philosophy of *sunyata* (Emptiness or Void). Otherwise stated, the spirit of the four elements just referred to comprising *cha-no-yu* concretizes the *prajna* philosophy of *sunyata*.

As a variation of the same theme, Horst Hammizsch[56] tells us in his own words that *cha-no-yu* is a way designed primarily by tradition to bring man to the annihilation of the ego, to pave the way for the ultimate experience of enlightenment, hence its unity with Zen (*chazen-ichima*). In other parlance, the true meaning of the Tea Ceremony's spirit is equally the true meaning of Zen spirit. Going into the four elements elaborated earlier on, reverence or *kei* while in favour of all living things is akin to deference, respect for other people, self-control. Harmony or *wa*, while revealing itself in one's personal behaviour, extends to one's relationship with one's whole environment and in one's adjustment to it. The combination of *kei* and *wa* ensures that deep feeling linking us to all other things, as it allows for participation at a really deep level of our being.

*Sei* or purity consists of an outer and inner cleanliness rooted in the naturally plain and simple; understood, too, in the moral-ethical-religious sense, it means readiness for the ultimate experience, to which the heart must surrender itself in all purity – free of emotions. *Jaku* or the element of tranquillity, while covering a whole range of deviation from its original meaning, is bound up with peace of heart, solitude demanding the avoidance of everything loud and obstructive, anything offending the eyes, hence its association with the ideal of beauty expressed by *wabi* and *sabi*, and with *sunyata* equally embracing silence.

In summation, it behoves Suzuki[9] to remark that *cha-no-yu* is not just drinking tea, but involves the entire atmosphere surrounding the procedure, the most important phase of which being the frame of mind or spirit which mysteriously grows out of the combination of the four elements referred to earlier on. The Tea Ceremony, therefore, is the art of cultivation what might be called 'psychosphere', or the psychic atmosphere, or inner field of consciousness akin to the spirit of poverty devoid of all forms of dichotomy: subject and object, good and evil, right and wrong, body and soul, gain and loss, and so on.

In keeping with what has been elaborated thus far, what follows next is unique in its kind and message, namely, the Zen landscape garden met principally in temples and monasteries, such as Ryoan-ji, which we have had the good fortune to visit years ago. While we have, no doubt, been quite impressed by it, we derive, to begin with, more satisfaction from, for instance, Watts' version of it[13]. Hence, the garden in question evokes an unbelievable simplicity bolstered by serenity and clarity of feeling so powerful that it can be caught even by photography. The major art or *bonseki* consists of five groups of rock laid upon a rectangle of raked sand, backed by a low stone wall and surrounded by trees, and enhanced by their moss-covered antiquity.

There are other views to be taken into consideration, such as those of Anne Bancroft[57] in that, while one is struck before anything else by the utter simplicity of the lay-out of the garden – a simplicity amidst just white sand, rocks and moss borne out of inner space merging into the outer one – the result is that inner and outer are fused into one. And again, while this is much more appreciated by those with some understanding of Zen, the aim of a Zen landscape garden 'is to bring alive in the spectator the meaning of the hidden essentials behind the appearances.' Laurens van der Post[58] takes the clue upon remarking that the Ryoan-ji is a garden 'before and beyond all gardens. It is self-denial of all means of eloquence at a garden's disposal, and leaving so much unsaid, it evokes a whole far more poignancy than any complex statement, however inspired, might have done.'

The Art of Flower Arrangement (*ikebana*) and the Noh-Theatre not coming into the picture here, the issue is extended to encompass the martial arts as the living expression of the Zen spirit in action. To this effect, Suzuki[9] informs us that one of the most significant features in the practice of martial arts is that they are not intended for utilitarian purposes only or for purely aesthetic enjoyment, but are meant 'to train the mind; indeed, to bring it into contact with ultimate reality'. In psychological terms, though, 'the mind has first to be attuned to the Unconscious', with the result that in the case of archery (*kyudo* or the Way of the Bow) the hitter and the hit are no longer two opposite objects, but one in reality.

Calling on Eugen Herrigel next[59] as an acknowledged Western master of *kyudo*, we are told that by 'archery in the traditional sense ... the Japanese does not understand a sport as such but, strange as it may sound at first, a religious ritual.' Hence, by the art of archery he does mean the ability of the sportsman, but an ability whose origin is to be sought in spiritual exercises and whose aim consists in hitting a spiritual goal, 'so that fundamentally the marksman aims at himself'. On the other hand, it is not true that, since

69

the traditional technique of archery is no longer important in fighting it has turned into a pleasant pastime, hence rendered innocuous.

On the contrary, one is dealing with the 'Great Doctrine' of archery telling us that 'it is a contest of the archer with himself; and this kind of contest is not a paltry substitute, but the foundation of all contests directed, for instance, with a bodily opponent. In this contest of the archer with himself is revealed a secret essence of this art, and instruction in it does not suppress anything essential by waiving the utilitarian ends to which the practice of knightly contest was put.'

Appraised at the mastership level, Herrigel has it that the contest consists in the archer himself – and yet not at himself – and thus becoming simultaneously the aimer and the aim, the hitter and hit, as Suzuki has intimated earlier on. Or, to use an expression nearest to the heart of the Japanese Master, it is necessary for the archer to become, in spite of himself, an unmoved centre. Then comes the supreme and ultimate miracle: art becomes artless, as it were; shooting become no-shooting, a shooting without bow and arrow; the teacher becomes the pupil again, the Master a beginner, and the beginning perfection. It means that the archer has by then cultivated the inner balance of mind and outer mastery of the body so that all movements arise without intervention of thought (read *wu-hsin* or *mushin*) translated by the absence of ego consciousness.

Lastly, while fencing or *kenso* falls outside the scope of this section, what retains our attention next is the art of swordsmanship which, as another martial art of note, is imbued with a similar spirit of Zen in action, yet with a difference. In effect, such a martial art or *kendo*, also known as *shimburyu* or *jimmu-ryu* (read,

70

the Way of the Sword), is set this time in a potentially lethal context, one, says Suzuki, which calls for a perfect presence of mind, the ability to react spontaneously (*jokiri*), and the fearless readiness to die. To wit, what makes swordsmanship closer to the spirit of Zen than any other martial art developed in Japan is that it involves the problem of death in the most threatening manner. It means that if one of the opponents makes one false movement he is doomed for ever: no time at all for conceptualized or calculated acts here.

In *kendo* everything that the opponent does must come right out of his inner mechanism, which is not under the control of consciousness. He must act instinctively and not intellectually. At the moment of most intense concentration relating to the struggle of life and death, what counts most is time and this must be utilized in the most effective way (read, the moment of intense concentration is the moment when a perfect identification takes place between the sword, the swordsman and his behaviour). When this is not reached, it means that the field of consciousness has not been completely cleared, there remaining a substrate of thought (*misai no ichisen*) which interferes with the act directly and straightforwardly issuing from the swordsman, that is, psychologically speaking, from the Unconscious.

# LOVE OF NATURE

The history of Zen has not only by tradition penetrated deeply into Japanese culture as we have just seen, but also into the Japanese love of nature, hence the necessity at the behest of Suzuki[9] of seeing the relationship between Zen and the Japanese love of nature. From the viewpoint of aesthetics, it means a kinship with a sense of asceticism as an essential feature in connection with the love of nature. Otherwise stated, with asceticism it consists in paying nature the fullest respect it deserves (read, treating nature not as an object to conquer and turn wantonly to our human service). In fact, Zen 'wants us to meet nature as a friendly, well-meaning agent whose inner being is thoroughly like our own, always ready to work in accord with our legitimate aspirations.' Zen asceticism consists in respecting nature and not violating her, irrespective of our own nature or the nature of the external world, adds the author. Zen recognizes that our nature is one with objective nature, in the sense that 'nature lives in us and we in nature'.

Having been inferred that the aesthetic aspect of Zen is closely related to asceticism, let it be said that there is in both the absence of selfhood and the merging of subject and object in one absolute emptiness or void (*sunyata*). This being the case, let us consider the aesthetic attitude of Zen towards objects in nature, the example of a flower from Suzuki[9] suiting admirably the purpose of this section. To begin with, most people do not really know how to look at the flower. For one thing they stand away from it, they never grasp the spirit of it. In other parlance, the one who beholds is separated from the object which is beheld, hence an impassable gap between them, the beholder unable to come in touch with his object in an inwardly manner, says he.

Encouraged in our quest for understanding, another important feature comes to the fore in that one ought to keep in mind that the experience of mere oneness is not enough for the real appreciation of nature. In effect, the merging, as it were, of self with others is absolutely necessary for the aesthetic comprehension of nature. For instance, the beauty of the aforesaid flower is readily appreciated only when it is referred to the ultimate reason of all things, neither in a mere philosophical and conceptual way, but in the way Zen proposes to accomplish it. That is, not in a pantheistic manner, nor in a quietistic fashion, but in the living way.

Still another feature finding acceptance here is that, contrarily to what could be thought, grasping the true Zen attitude toward nature spells neither an experience of identification, nor is it the feeling of the so-called 'eternal tranquillity' people often associate with it; worse, dream of it. To wit, the real flower is enjoyed only when the poet-artist lives with it, in it. The message is clear: the idea of 'eternal tranquillity' and that of identity between subject and object have to be shaken off.

The last topic with which we are concerned here has to do with transparency as keynote to the Zen understanding of nature, notwithstanding that, as Suzuki points out, it is from this that Zen love of nature stems for a start. As experience, transparency is not meant dualistically at all since, as long as one harbours conceptualization arising from the separation of subject and object and believes them final, 'the transparency is obscured and our love of Nature is contaminated with dualism and sophistry'.

Judging from the foregoing, it avers that what Zen is most anxious to do in its own characterization is to reject conceptual mediumship of any kind because 'any medium that is set up before Zen in its attempt to understand the facts of experience, is sure to obscure the nature of the latter'. Looking at it from an epistemological viewpoint, Suzuki[9] has it that Zen does not resort to the mediumship of concepts, but favours the doctrine of immediate grasping instead. From the Zen viewpoint it is to find an absolute point where no dualism is whatever forms obtains (read, owing to the doctrine of no grasping, Zen leads us into the realm of Emptiness or Void).

This brief excursion into the characterization of Zen attitude toward Nature is pregnant with another reminder in that it does not implicate a sense of identity, since, to the extent of repeating ourselves, for Zen there has never been any separation between subject and object. In fact, the aim of Zen 'is to restore the experience of original inseparability', meaning to return to the original state of purity and transparency. Neither is it a sense of tranquillity that Zen sees in nature because 'Nature is always in motion, never at a standstill; if Nature is to be lived, it must be caught while moving and in this way its aesthetic value must be appraised.' To seek tranquillity is to kill nature, to stop its pulsations, emphasizes Suzuki.

As we see it, part of the problem stems from man's isolation (some would have it alienation instead) from nature which, although we have evoked it at some length elsewhere[60], is reinforced by Watts[61] in that, contrarily to what is generally entertained, the isolation of the human soul from nature is, generally speaking, a phenomenon of civilization. Man persuades himself that he is a creator in his own right, separate from Nature. Bewitched by his power of reason and urged through 'fright or his fear man seeks his freedom in isolation from and not union with Nature – whose service is perfect freedom'. What the author is aiming at is that, as known to almost all the ancient people of the world and sages, having taught that all the actions of man were as much expressions of nature's unceasing movements as the sun and the wind, man is a meeting place for the interplay of forces from all quarters of the universe, 'swept through him in a stream which is the power behind all his thoughts and actions, which is indeed more truly that man's self than his body or mind.' With this we would totally agree.

Man's isolation from Mother Nature has induced Suzuki[9] to point further that the issue goes back to the Bible's account in which the Creator bestowed on the species the power to dominate all creation, hence the ensuing conquest of Nature. This idea of conquest coming from the relationship between Nature and man, and regarded as that of power, a state of mutual opposition and destruction, proves the result thereof. Such a power-relationship brings out the problem of rationality in that man is a rational being, while Nature is brutal; by logical inference, man strives to make nature amenable to his idea of rationality. On this showing, there is no discipline in Nature because it operates blindly; Nature is purposeless, and it is on account of this purposelessness that Nature is conquered by man.

It all goes to show that man himself is not man-made

75

but Nature-made, as much as anything we regard as of Nature. On the other hand, from a Zen viewpoint we hear that while separating himself from Nature, man is still a part of Nature, for 'the fact of separation itself shows that man is dependent on Nature.' Nature produces man out of herself; he still has its being rooted in Nature. From what has been gathered so far, there persists quite a gap between East and West in their respective approach to Nature, hence the need to go further into it.

Hence, while referring to still another *haiku* of the great Japanese poet Matsuo Basho,

> When I look carefully
> I see the *nazuma* blooming
> By the hedge!

Suzuki's comments strike us elsewhere[42] in that most Oriental poets feel every pulse of Nature. By contrast, most Westerners tend to alienate themselves from it on the ground that man and Nature have nothing in common except in some desirable aspects. But for Eastern people Nature is very close, so much that this feeling for Nature 'was stirred when Basho discovered an inconspicuous, almost negligible plant blooming by the old dilapidated hedge along the remote country road, so innocently, so unpretentious, not at all desiring to be noticed by anybody.' Yet when one looks for it, pursues the author, one feels as Basho did that even in every blade of wild grass, 'there is something really transcending all venal, base human feelings, which lifts one to the realm of the Pure Land (read, detecting something great in small things transcending all quantitative measurements)'.

At this point, though, the question is: 'What has the

West to offer in a similar situation?' Having selected for us Tennyson's well-known poem,[62] with something closely related to Basho's, here are Suzuki's remarks: the difference between the two poets is that Basho doesn't pluck the flower, he just looks at it. He is absorbed in the thought. He feels something in his mind, 'but does not express it. He lets an exclamation mark say everything he wants to say. For he has no reason to utter a single word; his feeling is too full, too deep, and he has no desire to conceptualize it.'

As regards Tennyson, he is the analyst and is active upon plucking the flower, hence separating it from the ground where it belongs; he doesn't leave the flower alone; he must tear it away, hence meaning that it must die. 'Apparently not caring for the plants' destiny, the curiosity of the famed poet is satisfied.' The message is clear: the East is silent while the West is eloquent. Yet the silence of the East does not mean just to be dumb and remain wordless and speechless. Silence in many instances is as eloquent as being wordy. The West, pursues Suzuki, likes verbalism. Not only that, the West transforms the word into flesh and makes this fleshiness come out into something too conspicuously, or rather too grossly voluptuously in its arts and religion (*sic*). In the case of the flower at issue, Tennyson's individuality stands away from the flower, from God and man; he does not identify himself with either of them. He is always apart from them. His understanding is of an objective nature while Basho's is thoroughly subjective in the sense that he sees the *nazuna* and the *nazuna* sees Basho. Here, notes the author, is no empathy, or sympathy, or identification for that matter: just mutual seeing. We may add that Basho being enlightened, the seer, the seen and the act of seeing become one.

# A QUESTION OF REALITY

Another piece of evidence bears on the acknowledged influence of Taoism on the mutation of Indian Buddhism into Zen, so much so that, according to Kakuo Okakura[63], Zen in Southern China incorporated much of Taoism. This was, incidentally, in keeping with the individualistic Southern mentality as opposed to the North of the country under the ethical spell of rigid Confucianism and correct societal etiquette. However, what concerns us here – in contrast to what has been elaborated thus far – is, so to speak, the exoteric aspect of Zen. In effect, the utter simplicity of Zen life and art – apart from gaining awakening or enlightenment – is not by any means getting away from the world, rather in coming back to it, and acting through it with love and compassion, in the words of Keido Kukushima Roshi. With this in mind, let us examine next what this exoteric aspect of Zen stands for within an epistemological and ontological context to lend cogency to the issue.

To begin with, and as already intimated, we in the West tend to regard the external or phenomenal world, the world 'out there' and us here as the result of our dualistic thinking or Cartesian heritage so rampant in our midst, hence the separation of self from the rest of the world, notwithstanding letting ourselves be caught in the web of opposites, pitting the ones against the others while blissfully unaware of the higher Heraclitean principle or Logos that contains and transcends them at the same time.

Contrarily to such a deplorable state of affairs likely to endure for an unspecifiable length of time still, the very notion that things and objects are taken 'out there' is, as we have seen, totally unacceptable to Zen. In fact, in contrast to the Platonic and Aristotelian system based on substance – or the philosophical system that recognizes in substance the most basic ontological element – Izutsu[51] remarks that Zen, ontologically speaking, is a system based on the category of relations or relatedness, that is, the idea that everything comes into being and exists as such in virtue of the infinite number of relations it bears to other things. In short, Zen ontology spells out an awareness of the essential interrelatedness and interdependence of all phenomena deprived of self-substance or self-subsistence.

What is evident at this stage is that, whereas Zen as 'philosophy' is one of interrelatedness and interdependence, Western substantialism sees in both the delineated ontological sphere of self-subsistent substance, their respective boundaries inalterably fixed and determined by their substance, in the words of Izutsu. Hence, subject and object are separated from one another as well as cut off from nature and the world. For Zen such a view is anathema, that is, 'it is locked in the magic circle of ontological dichotomy', and the only way of breaking such a spell is, as it were, by erasing ego-consciousness and unifying subject and object as well as the act of perceiving through non-dualism.

Other considerations begging similar priority of purpose, Suzuki[42] points out that Zen precedes and comes after our Western way of approaching reality. In other parlance, Zen is ante-scientific, even anti-scientifically so; in its connotative and ungrasping approach,

Zen takes life as it is instead of analyzing it into parts and dissecting it into bits and pieces. Preserving life as life, Zen 'plunges itself into the source of creativity and drinks from it all the life there is in it.'

Upon highlighting the foregoing it is clear that, while any description of Zen within the ambit of language is by no means that of Zen experience (read, at best a conceptualization in the way of language as its necessary vehicle), the same applies to ultimate reality. To wit, on the one hand, 'the roaring silence of the Buddha'; on the other hand, the description of reality itself referring to the phenomenon while saying nothing about the noumenon, as that lies much deeper than mere appearance. It follows that the constituents of description are not 'real' constituents of reality, rather those of language as has been altogether submitted.

In other words, reality is not what language portrays, the 'real' being a linguistic entity. The point is brought home even more forcibly by Zen, for whom language has no ontological significance when it comes to its relation with reality. In fact, Izutsu[51] reminds us that Zen recommends that words ought not to be clung to, since they have nothing to do with the nature of reality and, if so, but piecemeal only. To this effect, we may as well recall the injunction of philosopher Ludwig Wittgenstein that the word is not the thing, and the statement of semanticist Alfred Korzybski to the effect that the map is not the territory, to which we may add neither the score the music, the label the wine, and so forth.

At this point, if not attractively so, Christopher Titmuss[64] draws our attention that the teachings of Wittgenstein and of Nagarjuna well beforehand summon us to examine the way we take up views, cling to our belief in language games and imagine that any view of our identity and roles has inherent truth. The insights of these two thinkers of note appear in one sense to be obscure and abstract language games to which they would, of course, not agree. The message is clear: that such insights are profoundly valuable as deserving street credibility indeed.

To wit, in contrast to the Aristotelian or binary logic occupying a central position in our Western thought system, the quadripolarity of Nagarjuna with which we have, incidentally, dealt elsewhere[29], spells two further alternatives as mutually exclusive and jointly exhaustive: A is A and non-A; A is neither A nor non-A. However, such a quadripolarity (read, the four logical alternatives of Nagarjuna's dialectic) reportedly boasts of a fifth one as non-explicable ultimate reality by which is inferred *sunyata* (Emptiness or Void). It thus avers that from a Western viewpoint, Nagarjuna's first three alternatives (A is A; A is non-A; A is A and non-A) violate the principle of the excluded middle and of contradiction. As to the fourth alternative, A is neither A nor non-A, the laws of the excluded middle and of identity as altogether submitted by Izutsu[51]. Yet in all fairness to the famed philosopher and sage, notwithstanding his role as the 14th Patriarch of Zen in India, he accepted the validity of the law of the excluded middle in its purely logico-mathematical context, but not in the ontological framework as prime concern of metaphysics.

It is still significant that Nagarjuna's quadripolarity has been referred to by Erich Fromm[65] as paradoxical logic in that it assumes that A and non-A do not exclude each other as predicates of X, let alone that its predominance is met equally in Chuang-tzu, and Heraclitus. Woven around the same theme, we hear from Mark McDowell[66] that A is A and A is not not A

81

suit Western purposes in terms of philosophical discussions, while Nagarjuna's quadripolarity applies to non-Western considerations, the reason being that the Aristotelian law of the excluded middle occupies such a central position in Western thought in general, and its logical system in particular. Whereas it is easy for Western tradition to see that A is A and not non-A proves the only possibility, Nagarjuna's other two alternatives are in the same vein ruled out by the law of excluded middle, while altogether acceptable to Eastern thought as mutually exclusive and jointly exhaustive.

A similar piece of evidence emerges through Watts[47] in that at first sight Nagarjuna's quadripolarity seems to be a purely philosophical or intellectual endeavour, the object thereof being simply to refute any standpoint that may be forwarded. In fact, taken in a purely logical and academic sense, the Madhyamika or Middle school (read, which he founded) is the systematic refutation of any philosophical proposition: (i) A is; (ii) is not; (iii) both is and is not; (iv) neither is nor is not. From an ontological standpoint, though, we have: (i) being; (ii) not being; (iii) both being and non-being; (iv) neither being nor non-being. From a Western angle, pursues the author, (i) would assert St Thomas Aquinas' Being as Substance or the ultimate reality; (ii) not being dismissed by David Hume as the reification of a concept; (iii) both being and non-being stressing the mutuality in Georg W.F. Hegel's synthetic view of reality; (iv) neither being nor non-being suiting some sort of agnosticism or nihilism.

On the other hand, we might as well be reminded that, because language is dualistic or relational, any affirmation or denial whatsoever can have meaning only *vis-à-vis* its opposite. In fact, every statement, every definition, sets a boundary or limit; it classifies something and thus it can be shown by the same token that what is inside the boundary or limit must co-exist with what is outside. To be sure, even the idea of the boundless is meaningless without the contrast of the bounded or limited.

Watts comes to the conclusion that the intention of the Madhyamika or Middle school 'is not to create an infallible system of winning arguments. It is quite definitely a therapy, a liberative counter-game, and one of the historical antecedents of the technique of Zen.' Such an argument seems to us highly significant in that 'philosophizing' about Zen is centred, as we have seen, around the category of relatedness instead of substance in the Aristotelian tradition. The world of Zen is thus viewed from a relational standpoint, that is, the whole world of being where nothing is to be regarded as self-subsistent and self-sufficient.

In effect, the subject is subject because, as Izutsu[51] intimates, it is related to the object; the object is object on account of it being related to the subject. It follows that, at that point, Kant's famous dictum 'The thing-in-itself' is emphatically denied by Zen, or said not to exist at all for, among others, Watts in person. At any rate, reality for Zen is a relational web bereft of the dichotomy of Western intellect into subject and object. Zen is a concrete, freely articulated and self-differentiating field where no single object exists on its own.

Besides, the position of Zen, not to say its central notion of interrelationship, goes back to the Taoist view of nature as a seamless continuum of events, so also to the Buddha's early teachings which, in the words of Bede Griffiths[48], stressed that all phenomena are interrelated and are dynamic rather than static forms of interrelatedness. Whether one is dealing here with, incidentally, perhaps the reported leading epistemology of to-morrow, we find similar evidence for it way back to Dionysius the Areopagite (first century CE) in that the diversity of things exist not in separation but in a comprehensive unity whereby they are bound together in inseparable and everlasting unity.

Nearer to us philosopher Sarvepalli Radhakrishnan[67] not only does subscribe to the essential wholeness of reality underlying the world as ordered, unbroken unity, but sees nature as a system of relationships intimately interdependent: one large whole with matter, life, mind and values as its constituents, and while these remain utterly unlike each other, they yet intermingle and co-exist. Every existent is an organization with a special mode of relatedness. This, incidentally, ties up with the process metaphysics (read, organism or holism) of philosopher Alfred North Whitehead, according to which the world is a giant community whereby everything is influenced by everything else, 'there being nowhere a purely external single factor'.

This is also the case with the thesis of physicist David Bohm, spelling the connectedness of all things and events in a most fundamental yet primordial sense (read, wholeness). So also with the approach of scientist Erwin Laszlo, embracing the unifying pattern that underlies and connects things and events from which emerges a new concept of reality, according to which things are not recognized as separated nor events independent in the universe. So also the view of another physicist such as Gary Zukav, that in reality nothing is completely isolated, and all that presents itself is an unbroken wholeness or web of relationships. We could continue ...

It turns out that Peter Marshall[68] provides another striking example upon pointing out that Zen is profoundly libertarian as well as ecological, its goal being self-disciplined freedom or mental liberation from the chains of illusion, particularly the one for us humans of not being separate from Nature and the world. Like Buddhism, Zen stresses the admirable notion of *karuna* or compassion for all sentient beings.

However, in line with what has been previously remarked, that is, the influence of Taoism on the mutation of Indian Buddhism into Zen, it is felt warranted to mention that the first stirrings of an ecological sensibility were provided early by Taoists themselves. So much so that, as Marshall indicates once again, the early Taoists, opposed to the hierarchy of Confucian ethics and societal rules, offered a holistic worldview, recognizing the ecological principle of unity in diversity. Even more so, Taoists describe the world in a way strikingly similar to modern physics as a dance of energy within a boundless or seamless web, and as individuals realize themselves in relation to the whole. This brings us to the notion of age-old vintage shared by East and West alike, already alluded to[60], and coming under what Ken Wilber names the Integrative Vision.

# LIVING IN THE NO-BOUNDARY MOMENT

---

What is highly attributable here to our further understanding of Zen is that awakening or enlightenment,
remarks Suzuki[3], is beyond time; it is timeless, and Zen
has its *raison d'être* in timelessness. Moreover, the
author has it elsewhere[27] that we who are becoming in
time, must be able to see that which eternally is or
seeing the world *sub specie aeternatis* after Spinoza
(1632–77). What is implied here is living in the light of
eternity, by which is meant to get into the oneness and
allness of things and to live with it. This, incidentally,
is what the Japanese refers to as *sono-mama* or seeing
things in their suchness, and which rings the bell with
Blake's 'Hold infinity in the palm of your hand, and
eternity in an hour.' The message is clear: those who do
not know how to transcend time will naturally find it
difficult to attain Nirvana, which is eternity (read, the
unattainability of Nirvana comes from seeking it on
the other shore of becoming as if it were something
beyond time or birth-and-death).

Another customary insight from Suzuki[69] is worth
going into, in that time must merge into eternity, when
it gains its meaning, notwithstanding that time by itself
is nonexistent very much in the way that eternity is
impotent without time. Another pointer has it that in
our actual living in eternity the notion of time is
possible, even more so that each moment of living
marks the steps of eternity. It follows that to take hold

of eternity, consciousness must be awakened 'just at the very moment when eternity lifts its feet to step into time', as it were.

The question remains, though, how does *satori* fit into the picture? Various interpretations are in the offing; for one, when time is reduced to a point of no durability, it is absolute present or eternal now, *satori* being the experience of this fact; *satori* stands firmly on the absolute present, the eternal now; *satori* transcends time and space and their determinations, and is also in them. In terms of adequate further understanding of the issue, every moment we live is in eternity itself. The latter is no other than this instant. They are mutually merged and identical. This state of perfect interpenetration is the content of *satori*.

Calling on Watts once again for further light on the matter[61], he has it that eternity represented as unending time is not eternity but everlastingness in the sense that 'this kind of simplification may have its uses, but in many ways is an unnecessary complication for the conception has a greater value if we think of eternity as the timeless, eternal Now.' We hear elsewhere[70] that, from the standpoint of time, finite events are known successively; from the standpoint of eternity they are known simultaneously. Now, referring to timelessness or the strange sense of those timeless moments, Watts[13] intimates that it arises when one is no longer trying to resist the flow of events, the peculiar stillness and self-sufficiency of the succeeding instants when the mind, so to speak, is going along with them and not trying to arrest them.

So fundamental an issue warrants further testimony, hence the one of Zen Master Huang Po Hsi-yun (Jap: Obaku Kiun, d. 850), who used to repeatedly stress that eternity is right in front of us. Wilber[44] takes the cue upon saying that eternity is not awareness of everlasting time, but an awareness which itself is totally without time, that is, the eternal moment as a timeless moment, a moment which knows neither past nor future, before nor after, yesterday nor tomorrow, birth nor death. In other words, to live in and as the timeless moment is to live in what Wilber refers to as unity consciousness. In other parlance, most of us 'would have to admit that we have known moments, peak moments, which seemed indeed to lie far beyond time that the past and the future melted away in obscurity.'

Arguably, after all is said and done what about the time itself? A sound question that would, no doubt, suit the critical realist as it would entice him to explore the issue further, such a one being our mentor[52] for whom time is elusive, unattainable, so much so that if one tries to take hold of it by looking at it from the outside, then time is caught objectively in a serialism of past, present and future, it is like trying to touch one's own shadow. The unattainable must be grasped from the inside: one has to live in it and with it. On the other hand, writes Watts[13], if we open our eyes, we discover that the linear succession of time is a convention of our single-track verbal thinking, of a consciousness which interprets the world by grasping little pieces of it, calling them things and events. 'But every such grasp of the mind excludes the rest of the world, so that this type of consciousness can get an approximate vision of the whole only through a series of grasps, one after another.'

The foregoing speaking for itself, to merely admit that the notion of time down the centuries has given rise – and still does – to a good deal of controversy, or that to all intents and purposes no consensus can be reached on the issue, would be begging the question.

Hence, off the cuff: Heraclitus who, as is well-known, conceived of time as a flowing river in which one doesn't bathe twice. Nicolas of Cusa saw in time an enfoldment of eternity. William Blake interpreted time as a gift of eternity allowing us to live in succession. The poet Shelley referred to time as 'that unfathomable sea'. Philosopher Henri Bergson argued that time is invention (read, creation or intuition) or nothing. His famed predecessor, Kant, had it that time is but a form of one's sensitivity. Writer Paul Valéry proclaimed that time is construction, and Jorge Luis Borgès, another writer of note, that time isn't an immediate datum of consciousness, since it is ungraspable as the eye of the needle. Philosopher A.N. Whitehead asserted that it is impossible to meditate on time (and the creative passage of nature) without an overwhelming emotion of the limitation of human intelligence. Physicist David Bohm for his part opined that time is something our ideas do not cover very well. We could continue ...

On the strength of the evidence gathered so far, it would seem that the notion of time is not enjoying a consensus, probably never will, one reason proffered for it being that time remains something of a mystery, claiming its share of man's attention since the dawn of civilization, man in turn assuming a dimension quite its own without the dynamic pattern of time. As physicist Michael Shallis has it, time is one damn thing after another, yet despite being reminded by Zen Master Dogen Zenji to the effect that time does not pass (read, the idea of passing time may be called time but it is an incorrect one), it will not remove people's obsession with passing time, multifarious psychological and cultural influences coming into it, so also that one's own perception of time is, in the final analysis, incommunicable. Who knows if our three-dimensional mindset proves unequal to the task of coming to grips with the enigma of time, seeing that such a one appears to reside in the essence or quiddity of time itself?

# THIS SIDE OF THE EQUATION

What has been accounted for thus far points to our understanding of the spirit of Zen, in that its ultimate test is its effects on those who over the centuries put it into practice – and still do – for, as acknowledged, 'by their fruits ye shall know them' – yet not without some reservation here. In effect, many if not the majority in the West unfamiliar with or that much ignorant of Zen would, no doubt, query its purpose or even its value in bringing harmony into our society as a whole, notwithstanding the extent to which Zen could, in their view, improve social conditions, or the human lot for that matter. On the other hand, whereas Zen is definitely not the preserve of the chosen few, it couldn't be indiscriminately handed out to all and sundry, as Watts has it, with the exception being in favour of those who show themselves capable of understanding and applying its wisdom the right way. Another observation is this, though: contrary to knowledge, Zen is not power or something to be possessed for it has nothing to convey, yet somehow paradoxically, everything to live by in virtue of Zen wisdom is considered by its adepts as 'a most priceless of all treasures'. As has been remarked too, in order to obtain such wisdom a man must prove that he regards it as a sacred trust, never to be used for unworthy means.

Besides such mutually interpretative elements concerning Zen, no doubt applicable to ordinary life, we are reminded that, contrarily to other forms of Taoism,

Hinduism and Buddhism, Zen never had an esoteric or popular form. This is a moot point. Another notion worthy of our attention is the difficulty in following the Zen way because, as submitted by Powell[16], it is a path which is not of time and therefore not a 'way'. Quite so, albeit that in another parlance one doesn't 'get by' Zen; one experiences it right through, until awakening or enlightenment is attained across the 'pathless path', or, through the 'gateless gate'.

Such an understanding helps, no doubt, a good deal, yet it would prove of momentary value unless, as process, it is experienced anew without the intervention of the ego, or memory for that matter. It means that, once the essential unreality of the ego has been acknowledged as, moreover, squashed at both conscious and unconscious levels, a genuine ongoing transformation is in the offing, that is, in the form of discovering one's true, original Buddha nature. At that point we may recall that the dualism of thinker and thought, subject/object, is no more; better still, when thinker, thought and the act of thinking are no more separated.

Watts expresses it succinctly here, in that 'the individual no more feels himself to be standing back from his sensation of the world, just as he is no longer a thinker standing back from his thoughts.' In other parlance, such a one has a vivid sense of himself as identical with what he sees and hears; he is not so much an organism in an environment as 'an organism-environment relationship'. The one who has realized this unity is no longer a trap to catch itself.

To pursue, the proper understanding and practice of Zen are means for setting man free from his own crutches, as made distinct from the collection of individuals divided – as is the rule – from each other, as alienated from the rest of the world. And while it falls outside the scope of this section to indicate the prerequisites for bringing about a change of attitude in man's relationship with his fellow-men and Nature, what is needed is the man who, irrespective of his background, is steeped in Zen consciousness. A cautionary remark here in that this would not herald a new sort of consciousness, yet one that transcends the exclusive rational and discursive, materialistic and reductionistic thinking still dominant in our midst, notwithstanding that intellection and rationalism – while decisively ruling the post-modern era – leave little room for the intuitive.

To this effect, the aim is not trying to build a bridge between East and West, since Zen consciousness in its universality and unity knows no boundary, rather more truly human in the wake of an out-of-the-ordinary spiritual discipline providing us with the stability and sanity needed more than ever in that so human and yet confusing world of ours, we are told. In breaking forth from the I-me-mine syndrome, from dualistic thinking and beyond the opposites, Zen consciousness affords an opening borne afresh to the breadth and fullness of our being, as shorn of any elitist otherworldliness to boot.

Another piece of evidence is that, caught in conceptually passing time, our civilization is reportedly not geared to the highly desirable all-embracing perception of the essence or quiddity of things in the wake of Zen teaching, let alone within some kind of integral consciousness spelling transparency and holistic experience beyond conceptually linear time. Little wonder, then, that Zen comes appropriately to the fore in its ability to penetrate, beyond concepts and beyond verbalism, down to the essence or quiddity of things underlying them, yet without eliminating them.

After all, as Keido Kukushima Roshi observes, Zen is not just a matter of gaining enlightenment; it is a matter of acting in a world of love and compassion. Besides, doesn't it spell an invitation to a life born anew in its otherness? Doesn't it mean to realize one's existence in the lucidity of the here and now as, on both counts, letting life unravel its own simplicity in a most extraordinary manner? We would think so through what Zen has to offer. In this respect, the latter has been aptly said to be a way to our long-lost home (read, a homeward way to one's original, true or Buddha nature).

What we encounter here is that to negotiate such a way demanded of us by Zen doesn't necessitate to call oneself a Zen adept, rather as one 'abiding nowhere' in the wake of the *Diamond Sutra*[71]. In effect, whereas the way of Zen turns out to be a way to an end, it is in reality a way without an end, as has been judiciously pointed out, yet around the necessity to look to oneself for inner liberation (read, while not depending upon others for the purpose). And again, besides getting rid of the delusion of the ego, this calls for forfeiting the ingrained lure of our perceptions, our discursive linear thinking, knowing ourselves and our world through a thick filter of heresies and analytical reasoning, in the worlds of John Daishin Buksbazen[72]. It means putting a stop to splitting ourselves and the world (read, the world we still take to be 'out there'), but grasping reality in a direct, unmediated manner.

This in our estimation has a most significant value in that, furthermore, it means reaching out for the inner-most depths of ourselves, our identity with existence itself, ideas and symbols, as Watts has it[3], replaced by direct, non-conceptual touch with level of being which is simultaneously one's own and the being of all others.

94

To wit, 'At the point where I am most myself I am most beyond myself. At root I am one with all the other branches. Yet this level of being is not something to be grasped and categorized ... because it is a point from which one radiates, the light not before but within the eyes.'

Such a view finds an equal implicity with R.H. Blyth[74] for whom Zen is not only a way of liberation as already inferred, but also a way of disentangling ourselves from the social level of masks and role-playing, which, he says, we have mistaken for our identity. For the purpose of Zen is the opening of the eye of insight or enlightenment that cuts through the crust of verbal knowledge and reveals the underlying and inseparability of the individual and the universe (read, back to the Integrative Vision[60]).

Through confusing words and abstractions with reality, pursues the author, 'we have created an artificial role of personality for ourselves and in the process forgotten that it is just a role and not the real source of our actions.' What it boils down to is that society has tricked us into the belief that one's mind is inside one's head and acts independently from it at the same time that 'it is also telling us who we are and what we should be doing.' Here is the rub, though: 'since the mind then includes all of one's social relationships, it is not inside the skin of the individual at all but is actually outside it.'

Here are other points raised by Hubert Benoit[75] in connection with the existentialism of Zen. To begin with, man in general feels that 'living' is superior to 'existing', such an opinion so clear-cut, so entranched that he ends up in regarding existing as nothing much, and living everything. Yet the distinction between these two terms being such that it often cancels itself out:

existing is taken for living and vice versa. Hence, living appears so uniquely important for man that the very expression 'existing' is deprived of its true meaning. Man fulfils 'existing' only because it is a mandatory condition of living: he exists in order to live, thus going against the grain of the established order of things. At this stage, we are being reminded that 'existing' stems from the Latin *ex-stare* (outside of); moreover, the term enjoys a universal status as the centrifugal impetus of Being. As regards the egotist drive of living, though, it does not subscribe to the relative reality of existing. In other parlance, the illusory belief in the reality of individual living is founded on the ignorance of the universal existing.

Wishing to bring the argument further home, Benoit has it that the attainment of *satori* is nothing else but the full awareness of the existing actually unconscious within oneself. In other words, *satori* not as consciousness born *ex nihilo* but as a metaphor of mediate consciousness into immediate consciousness. The author can thus afford to say that he is not directly conscious of his own existence, that is, his existing self, but only of the phenomenal variations of that very existence of his. And it is his own present belief in the absolute reality of those variations which separate him from the consciousness of what actually underlies them (read, which do not vary, noumenal existence, principle of his phenomenal existence).

Now, it is part of man's condition to go through the desire of existing in order to reach out for the existential consciousness that will abolish that very desire, yet not to the point of being the slave thereof which Zen denounces. Man has to go through the illusory living in order to reach the real existing on the ground that existing precedes living in the sense that the principle precedes by necessity its manifestation. Another reminder from Benoit elsewhere[76] is worth going into in that 'Zen tells man that he is free, that no chain exists which he needs to throw off; he has only illusions of the chain.' In other parlance, man will enjoy his freedom as soon as he ceases to believe that he needs to free himself, as soon as he 'throws from his shoulders the terrible duty of salvation'. This, incidentally, enjoins the famous Zen saying – no doubt among many others – 'Do not put any head above your own!'

# THE GOOSE IS OUT

There was a time when it was thought that Zen was not meant for Western consumption, C.G. Jung in the lead if we recall rightly, no doubt among many others of similar persuasion[77]. Yet time has since then established that Zen has been made largely accessible to our part of the world, notwithstanding that it is gathering momentum in many quarters. Admittedly, an essential form of mainstream Buddhism as reportedly the most important experience of human history, so to speak, Zen moreover stands on its own as the acknowledged flower or apothesis of Buddhism. To be sure, though, the West on the whole remains influenced by an old if not paradoxical provincialism *vis-à-vis* Eastern wisdom, we are told, considering that less than one century and a half separates us from Schopenhauer, the first Western philosopher who, it is said, tried to interpret the message of Buddhism as a living, enriching doctrine whose origin goes back some 2,500 years ago after Shakyamuni Buddha, the Awakened One.

The nature of the foregoing raises the question of Western tradition as such, hence the explanation of William Barrett[78] to the effect that the tradition in question is the outcome of a twin heritage through the major influences of the Hebrews and Classical Greece impregnated with a profound spirit of dualism. That is, the former on both religious and moral grounds (read, dualism between God and his creatures, Moral Law and its fallible servants, spirit and flesh); division of reality on the intellectual level, of the world of intellection and that of the senses in the case of the latter. It means that the momentous contribution of Classical Greece has been to define the rationalist ideal of man, to the extent of making reason the highest and noblest human function, if not the centre of personality. For their part, though, Easterners have never fallen for it in that, pursues Barrett, upon putting intuition above reason, they have offered personality a focus whereby the conflicting contradictions between reason and the irrational, intellection and the senses, ethics and nature are abolished, those very dualities that we in the West have inherited.

While the author points out that Zen has nothing to do with Western disciplines – be they philosophical, scientific, cultural or aesthetic – since they deal with the complex abstractions of intellectualism, the present essay has shown that what Zen looks for above everything else are concrete and simple things precisely beyond the tangled complexities of intellectualism. Zen avoids complexities, or makes use of them with a view to overstepping them. Zen is concreteness itself; in fact, its signification goes well beyond simple conceptualization, its language being one with its subject. Zen is all for the living fact, as in keeping with its intention of rendering the individual quite naked, casting off all his rags in order to give him back to himself. And this is in our eyes perhaps one of the most revealing features of Zen which, in its reported individuality compounded at times of iconoclastic and paradoxical elements, remains nevertheless an endeavour meant for the whole man in all he totally undertakes and which, brought to fruition, is 'one of the most haunting and subtle spiritual traditions in the world'.

This being said, it is clear that for those in the West

seeking enlightenment the waking state is Zen's essence as much as its goal, yet upon the understanding that, as has been aptly remarked, the whole point is not to alter Zen in order to suit Western requirements, rather making Zen amenable to the West. This, incidentally, is what such eminent exponents as Suzuki, Blyth, Merton and Watts – no doubt among others – have achieved to their lasting credit, namely, as universal experience stemming from a higher yet renewed level of consciousness.

Zen is the game of intuitive insight brought to fruition, the game of discovering our true or Buddha nature through, we are told by Sohl and Carr[74], the role we are playing, hence becoming aware of the real actor behind the mask. Moreover, as has been indicated too, Zen is taken as the very essence of life itself, the very merging of opposites in which man finds himself at one with the universe, meaning that in such a case we have nothing outside ourselves to gain.

Zen comes into the picture as direct, unmediated, non-conceptualized experience not limited to the dualistic nature of language once we cease confusing the indivisible nature of reality with the differentiation and conceptual pigeonholes of language, however sophisticated. Zen as extension of our own consciousness helps us, perhaps for the first time, to see things as they are, that is, beyond the shadows on the wall evoked by Plato's simile of the Cave. Hence, reaching the waking state implies an undifferentiated state where subject and object are one: words do not express things (read, they express words), things express things and not so by words, as Blyth has it.

Such a compelling distinction encourages us to pursue, in that Zen is something which can neither be given nor received nor transmitted, on the ground that, as intimated earlier on by Watts, Zen is not a 'what'. Hence the mistake of looking for Zen, whose very life – or spirit for that matter – is so difficult to be inculcated, there being, besides, nothing to 'know' about it in the deepest sense of the word. Arguably, though, how to define Zen other than has been submitted in this essay; how to talk with or about it? Appealing, once again, to Blyth for an appropriate answer, we hear that we get a ladleful of it here and there according to our innate abilities, and our opportunities somehow accidentally on both counts. Now, to talk with Zen is not uncommon, and talking about Zen is more common than it should be, but to talk with Zen about Zen is the rarest thing in the world.

We feel grateful to the author upon being reminded, next, that Zen is common life and uncommon life, sense and transcendence, both as one, yet two. Zen, says he, 'is a word that is used like an algebraic sign, for all that is nameless, all that escapes thought, definition, explanation, yet is communicated in spite of our best efforts to communicate it.' To which we would add for the benefit of the reader not tutored in the Zen discipline:

> The present essay is like a finger
> pointing at Zen, hence perish the
> thought that it be mistaken for Zen
> itself!

# REFERENCES AND NOTES

1. Alan Watts: *Beat Zen, Square Zen*, City Lights Books, San Francisco, 1959
2. Deisetz T. Suzuki: *Zen and Japanese Buddhism*, Japan Travel Bureau Inc, Tokyo, 1968
3. —: *The Field of Zen*, The Buddhist Society, London, 1980
4. Thomas Merton: *Zen and the Birds of Appetite*, New Direction Books, New York, 1968
5. Alan Watts: *The Spirit of Zen: A Way of Life, Work and Art in the Far East*, John Murray, London, 1972
6. —: *Zen Buddhism: A New Outline and Introduction*, The Buddhist Society, London, 1947
7. Karlfried von Dürckheim: *Le Zen et Nous*, Le Courrier du Livre, Paris, 1976
8. Sohatu Ogata: *Zen For the West*, Tider, London, 1959
9. Deisetz T. Suzuki: *Zen and Japanese Culture*, Pantheon Books Inc, New York, 1960
10. Thomas Merton: *Zen Revival*, The Buddhist Society, London
11. Toshihito Isutzu: 'Meditation and Intellection in Japanese Zen Buddhism' in *Traditional Modes of Contemplation and Action*, edited by Yusuf Ibish and Peter Lamborn Wilson, Imperial Iranian Academy of Philosophy, Tehran, 1977
12. Christmas Humphreys: *Zen Comes West*, Hodder & Stoughton, London, 1981
13. Alan Watts: *The Way of Zen*, Thames & Hudson, London, 1958
14. Philip Kapleau: *Zen: Dawn in the West*, Rider, London, 1980
15. Richard De Martino: *The Human Situation and Zen cf Zen Buddhism and Psychoanalysis* in co-authorship with Deisetz T. Suzuki and Erich Fromm, George Allen and Unwin, London, 1960
16. Robert Powell: *Zen and Reality*, Penguin Books, London, 1978
17. Aldous Huxley: *Island*, Bantam, New York, 1960

18. Robert Pirsig: *Zen and the Art of Motorcycle Maintenance*, Corgi Books, London, 1978
19. M. Conrad Hyers: *Zen and the Comic Spirit*, Rider, London, 1973
20. Warwick Fox: *Towards a Transpersonal Ecology: Developing New Foundations for Environmentalism*, Shambhala, Boston & London, 1990
21. Matthieu Ricard: *Le Moine et le Philosophe* in co-authorship with Jean-François Revel, *Le Bouddhisme Aujourd'hui*, NIL Editions, Paris, 1997
22. Deisetz T. Suzuki: *The Awakening of Zen*, Prajna Press, Boulder, Colorado, 1980 in association with the Buddhist Society, London
23. —: *Essays in Zen Buddhism (1st Series)*, Rider, London, 1958
24. Ernest Wood: *Zen Dictionary*, Penguin, London, 1977
25. Alan Watts: *The Two Hands of God; The Myths of Polarity*, Rider, London, 1978
26. Deisetz T. Suzuki: *Manual of Zen Buddhism*, Rider, London, 1950
27. —: *Essays in Zen Buddhism (Third Series)*, Rider, London, 1953
28. Christmas Humphreys: *Zen, A Way of Life*, Hodder & Stoughton, London, 1981
29. M.J. de Mallac: *Western Paths, Eastern Paths: An Exploration of Reality*, The Book Guild, Lewes, 1997
30. Pierre Thuilier: *La Grande Implosion. Rapport sur l'Effrondement de l'Occident, 1999–2001*, Fayard, Paris, 1995
31. Robert Hamilton: *Earthdream: The Marriage of Reason and Intuition*, Green Books, Devon, 1990
32. Aldous Huxley: *The Perennial Philosophy*, Chatto & Windus, London, 1950
33. Ken Wilber: *The Eye of the Spirit: An Integral Vision for a World Gone Slightly Mad*, Shambhala, Boston & London, 1987
34. Deisetz T. Suzuki: *What is Zen?*, The Buddhist Society, London, 1971
35. Thomas Cleary: *Zen Essence: The Science of Freedom*, Shambhala, Boston & Shaftesbury, 1989
36. Toshihiko Izutsu: *Toward a Philosophy of Zen Buddhism*, Imperial Iranian Academy of Philosophy, Tehran, 1977

37. John Polkinghorne: *Science and Creation: New Science Library*, Shambhala, Boston & London, 1989
38. Alan Watts: *Tao: The Watercourse Way*, with the collaboration of Al Chung-Huang, Jonathan Cape, London, 1975
39. F.C. Happold: *Mysticism: A Study and An Anthology*, Penguin Books, London, 1979
40. Ken Wilber: *No Boundary: Eastern and Western Approaches to Personal Growth*, Shambhala, Boulder & London, 1981
41. *The Holographic Paradigm and Other Paradoxes: Exploring the Leading Edge of Science*, edited by Ken Wilber, Shambhala, Boulder & London, 1981
42. Roger Walsh: *Staying Alive: The Psychology of Human Survival. New Science Library*, Shambhala, Boulder & London, 1985
43. Deisetz T. Suzuki: *Lectures on Zen Buddhism cf Zen Buddhism and Psychoanalysis* in collaboration with Erich Fromm and Richard De Martino, George Allen & Unwin, London, 1960
44. *The Diamond Sutra* and the *Sutra of Hui-Neng*, translated by A.F. Price and Wong Mou-Lam, Shambhala, Boulder, 1969
45. Ken Wilber: *Up From Eden: A Transpersonal View of Human Evolution*, Shambhala, Boulder, 1983
46. Chandradhar Sharma: *A Critical Survey of Indian Philosophy*, Rider, London, 1960
47. Renée Weber: *Dialogues With Scientists and Sages*, Arkana, London, 1990
48. Alan Watts: *Psychotherapy East and West*, Penguin Books, London, 1973
49. Bede Griffiths: *A New Vision of Reality: Modern Science, Eastern Mysticism, and Christian Faith*, Fount/Harper Collins, London, 1992
50. Thomas Merton: *The Way of Chuang-tzu*, Unwin Books, London, 1975
51. From the *Hsin Hsin Ming Verses on the Faith Mind* by Sosan Zenji, cf *The Heart Never Sleeps: Striking to the Heart of Zen* by Dennis Genpo Merzel, Shambhala, Boston & London, 1991
52. Deisetz T. Suzuki: *Studies in Zen*, Rider, London, 1957
53. George Steiner, *A George Steiner Reader*, Penguin Books, London, 1984

54. Alan Watts: *Zen Buddhism: A New Outline and Introduction*, The Buddhist Society, London, 1947
55. Philip Rawson and Laszlo Legaza: *Tao: The Chinese Philosophy of Time and Change*, Thames & Hudson, London, 1983
56. Horst Hammitzsch: *Zen and the Art of the Tea Ceremony*, Arkana, London, 1993
57. Anne Bancroft: *Zen, Direct Pointing to Reality*, Thames & Hudson, London, 1979
58. Laurens van der Post: *Yet Being Someone Other*, The Hogarth Press, London, 1982
59. Eugen Herrigel: *Zen and the Art of Archery*, Arkana, London, 1985
60. To wit:

The Eternal Tao in its ontological meaning is an inner experience whereby man and the universe interpenetrate each other.

The Taoist notion whereby the observer is an integral part of the web of existence, and existence is part of the universe.

The Confucian metaphysics is one of anthropocentric unity in that Heaven and man are an inseparable oneness.

The Chinese trend of thought has it that man is a cosmos in miniature and is not divided from the great cosmos by any fixed limit, after Sinologist Richard Wilhem.

'I and all things in the universe are one!' (Chuang-tzu, c.369–286 BCE)

'Heaven and Earth and I are of the same root/ The ten thousand things and I are one substance.' (Sojo, noted Zen monk and scholar of T'Ang dynasty China)

'The very small is as the very large when boundaries are forgotten; the very large is as the very small when its outline is not seen.' (Seng-ts'an, noted Zen scholar, sixth century CE)

The Vedic-Upanishadic tradition according to which man is not separate from the universe through the Brahman-Atman self-identification.

The universe is synthetized, concretized in man. (*Arharva Upanishad*)

'I am this world and eat this world. Who knows it, knows.' (*Taittireeya Upanishad*)

The Hermetic dictum 'As above, so below' linking the microcosm and the macrocosmos, nature and man, and the observer with the observed, in the words of Renée Weber of Princeton.

The great gift of the Nondual Tradition according to which we and the cosmos are of one Spirit.

The core of mystical consciousness spelling man's baptismal union with the universe.

'We ourselves are even another little world, and having within us the sun and the stars.' (Origen, c.254–185 BCE)

Each human being contains in himself the whole world according to Plotinus (270–205 BCE).

Man is a mirror of the cosmic order after Giordano Bruno (1548–1600).

'Man is the whole world, and the breath of God.' (Sir Thomas Browne, 1605–82)

'Humans are the soul of the universe and participate in the transformation of Heaven and Earth.' (Kaibaro Ekken, 1630–1713)

For Spinoza (1632–77) God and Nature are an interchangeable reality, hence reflecting the Hindu notion of Brahman-Atman.

'You never enjoy the world alright, till the Sea itself floweth in your veins, till you are clothed with the heavens, and crowned with the stars; and perceive yourself to be the sole heir of the whole world, and more than so, because men are in it who are every sole heirs as well as you.' (Thomas Traherne, 1636–74)

'Man bears the whole universe within himself and comes

closest to the mystery of the world by stepping inside himself.' (Friedrich Wilhem von Schelling, 1875–1961)

'We are the world, and the world is in us.' (Alfred North Whitehead, 1861–1947)

'We are the universe, in every fibre of our body and being, nerve and thought.' (William McNeil-Dixon, 1866–1946)

Awareness of man's intimate relationship with life and the cosmos itself subsumes a feeling of wholeness after Carl Gustav Jung (1875–1961).

'We live our lives incrustably within the streaming mutual life of the universe.' (Martin Buber, 1878–1965)

'Man is part of the whole we call Universe.' (Albert Einstein, 1879–1955)

'Man is made up of what the world is made up.' (Ramana Maharshi, 1879–1950)

The human phenomenon as part of the cosmic process itself in the view of Pierre Teilhard de Chardin (1881–1955).

'Not only the universe surrounds me, it penetrates me.' (J.B.S. Haldane, 1892–1964)

'The world is not separate from us; we are the world, and our problems are the world's problems.' (J. Krishnamurti, 1895–1986)

'Most of us have lost the sense of unity of biosphere and humanity.' (Gregory Bateson, 1904–80)

'Zen reveals the underlying and inseparable reality of the individual and the universe.' (R.H. Blyth, 1898–1964)

'Today in science, the universe is a field of energies, working at different frequencies, and we are all parts of this field of energies. We are connected in it as part of our being.' (Bede Griffiths, 1906–92)

'The human organism is a continuous process with all the universe.' (Alan Watts, 1915–73)

'We are enfolded in the universe, and all our experience is a clue to reality because we are reality.' (David Bohm, 1917–92)

'Forging self, the Universe grows I.' (Edwin Arnold)

We are the ears and eyes of the universe after Joseph Campbell.

The universe reflects itself in man not only physically, but psychically according to G. Formichi.

'From a transpersonal viewpoint, one feels at one with the world, or has a sense of unity of everything, and the universe.' (Abraham Maslow)

'We are made of the stuff of the universe itself ... We are co-extensive with the universe through every pore of our skin, through every fragment that makes us up.' (Jean Charron)

'We are unbounded, part of a greater wholeness, united with the rest of the universe ... This is the other side of our identity.' (Peter Russell)

'Nothing happens in isolation, everything is tied up with cosmic clues. Life on planet Earth is united into what amounts to be a single superorganism, and this in turn is only part of the cosmic community.' (Lyall Watson)

'The fully developed human being is understood to be the integration of all purposes and energies of cosmic nature.' (Jacob Needleman)

'We are mysteriously connected with the entire universe, we are mirrored in it, just as the entire evolution of the universe is mirrored in us.' (Vaclav Havel)

'We are members of the great universe community. We participate in its life. We are nourished by this community, we are instructed by this community, we are healed by this community.' (Thomas Berry)

'After all, there is one world, and we are part of it.' (Larry Dossey)

'We are embodied participants in the co-creation of our

world. The human mind makes its world by participating in its being.' (Peter Reason)

To accept the world, remarks Maurice Ash, is to be part of it oneself.

Quantum mechanics shows that we are not separated from the world as one thought; in fact, we are part of the readout, as pointed out by such physicists as Fritjof Capra, Gary Zukav, Jeremy Hayward, Alan Wallace among, no doubt, others.

'We are the universe itself, its consciousness, its intelligence.' (Jean Guitton)

'The integrative perspective or unifying pattern that underlies and connects things and events calls for apprehending environment, nature and the universe as a whole.' (Erwin Laszlo)

'There is no rupture between the universe and man who is part of it.' (Jean d'Ormesson)

'We and the entire universe are one state or one experience; one is not entering this state, rather it is a state which, in some profound and mysterious way, has been one's primordial condition since time immemorial. One has never left this state at all, not even for a second.' (Ken Wilbur)

'We desperately need to find our way back to wholeness ... (since) everything seems to interact with everything else at some subtle levels of the Universe beyond the purely physical level, and the deeper we penetrate into these other levels, the more do we realize that we are One.' (William Tiller)

'We are living in a participatory universe, and the interrelatedness of human consciousness and the observed world implies that we cannot be regarded as distinct, separate entities.' (John Archibald Wheeler)

'Newton's vision tore us up out of the fabric of the universe.' (Danah Zohar)

'The universe is all inclusive and includes us; we are part of

110

and an aspect of the universe experiencing and thinking about itself.' (Edward Harrison)

'Body and mind should be one, unified with the activity of the universe.' (Morihei Ueshida)

'Our bodies are part of the universal body, our minds an aspect of universal mind.' (Deepak Chopra)

'If we are, indeed, creatures of the Cosmos, as modern evidence is tending to show, would it not seem reasonable that we have some innate intuition of the nature of the cosmos itself hidden deep within ourselves? A relationship between the microcosm of life and the Universe at large must exist for the simple reason that the one is derived from the other.' (Chandra Wickramsinghe)

(From the present writer's *Western Paths, Eastern Paths: An Exploration of Reality*, The Book Guild, Lewes, 1997)

61. Alan Watts: *The Meaning of Happiness: The Quest for Freedom in the Spirit of Modern Psychology and the Wisdom of the East*, Rider, London, 1978
62. Flower in the crannied wall,
    I pluck you off the crannies: –
    Hold you there, root and all, in my hand,
    Little flower – but if I could understand
    What you are, root and all, and all in all
    I should know what God and man is.'
63. Kakuo Okakura: *The Book of Tea Ceremony*, Shambhala Pocket Classics, Boston & London, 1993
64. Christopher Titmuss: *The Green Buddha*, Insight Books, Devon, 1995
65. Erich Fromm: *Psychoanalysis and Zen cf Zen Buddhism and Psychoanalysis* in conjunction with Deisetz T. Suzuki and Richard De Martino, George Allen and Unwin, London, 1960
66. Mark McDowell: *A Comparative Study of Don Juan and Madhyamika Buddhism*, Motilal Banarsidas, Bombay, 1981
67. Sarvepalli Rhadakrishnan: *An Idealist View of Life*, Unwin Books, London, 1961
68. Peter Marshall: *Nature's Web: An Exploration of Ecological Thinking*, Simon & Schuster, London, 1992

69. Deisetz T. Suzuki: *Living by Zen*, Rider, London, 1972
70. Alan Watts: *The Supreme Identity: An Essay on Oriental Metaphysics and the Christian Religion*, Wildhouse, London, 1973
71. Literally: 'Sutra of the Diamond-Cutter of Supreme Wisdom', an independent part of the *Prajnaparamita-sutra*, which attained great importance, particularly in East Asia; *The Encyclopaedia of Eastern Philosophy and Religion: Buddhism, Taoism, Hinduism*, Shambhala, Boston, 1994
72. John Daishin Buksbazen: *To Forget the Self: An Illustrated Guide to Zen Meditation*, Zen Centre of Los Angeles, 1977
73. Alan Watts: *Beyond Theology, The Gospel According to Zen*, Mentor Books/New American Library, New York, 1970
74. *Games Zen Masters Play. Writings of R.N. Blyth*, selected and edited by Robert Sohl and Audrey Carr, Mentor Books/New American Library, New York, 1976
75. Hubert Benoit: *La Doctrine Suprême selon le Zen*, La Colombe, Editions du Vieux Colombier, Paris, 1960
76. —: *Salvation or Satori, The Gospel According to Zen*, Mentor Books, The New American Library, New York, 1970
77. A typical case in point emanates from Arthur Koestler for whom Zen is a deliberately amoral (*sic*), and illogical antidote to the rigours of 'a hierarchic, cramped, self-conscious society in medieval Japan and earlier on in China.' And again, in the form in which it is taught and practised today, 'Zen spells intellectual and moral nihilism', and this for two reasons. First, the emphasis is not on marrying intuition to reason, but on castrating reason. Second, Zen's moral detachment has degenerated into complacency towards, and complicity with, evil (*sic*). The message is clear: the Western intelligentsia is advised to recognize contemporary Zen as 'one of the sick jokes, slightly gangrenous at that, while always fashionable in ages of crisis.' (*Bricks to Babel*, Picador, London, 1982)
78. William Barrett: *Zen Pour L'Occident. Le Monde du Zen. Anthologie du Bouddhisme Zen composée et présentée par Nancy Wilson Ross*, Stock, Paris, 1960